PATCHES PARTY

TOGAS

Toga parties are the best fun around. Simply wrap yourself in a sheet and nowt much else. Remember to fasten the safety pins, though!!

Sheets by British Home Stores.

For the best way to have a pyjama party, turn to the back pages of your annual.

£2·55

what's INSIDE

Printed and published by
D. C. Thomson & Co., Ltd.,
185 Fleet Street, London EC4A 2HS.
© D. C. Thomson & Co., Ltd., 1985.

ISBN 0 85116 330 0

PAtCHEs BeaUTY CALeNdar

BEAUTY (vertical text in left margin)

JANUARY

CLEAN IT UP!

No matter how perfect your skin, January is a month when everyone suffers! It can't be helped really — you've got to face those freezing winds and the drying-out effects of central heating. So, whatever your skin type, you need all the protection you can get.

Dry Skin roughens easily, it may even flake, and feels distinctly tight and dry after washing. Clean it gently with creamy cleansers or lotions, and treat yourself to regular applications of moisturiser — worked in carefully with your fingertips. Apply a heavy moisturiser at night — Oil of Ulay Night Cream is good — and blot off the excess with a tissue before getting into bed. Remember to apply moisturiser under your make-up — it helps protect your face, and try Boots No. 7 Colour Corrective if your cheeks get very red in the cold.

Oily Skin needs soap and water, astringent if it's especially bad, and a light moisturiser. Choose a moisturiser like Simple which has no perfumes or irritants and massage it lightly in after washing. If wearing a moisturiser under your make-up makes your face look shiny, try a foundation with a built-in moisturiser to avoid this — and brush translucent powder lightly over it afterwards to make doubly sure.

Combination Skin — the commonest skin type, usually consisting of an oily T-shaped area — the forehead, nose and chin — and dry cheeks. Treat combination skin as if it was two different types — deeply

cleansing and toning the oily section and gently cleansing and moisturising the dry areas. Use a light moisturiser all over the face to protect it from the worst of the elements, but apply it sparingly on the oily area and generously over the dry cheeks.

FEBRUARY

FINGER TIPS!

This is the month to make all those long, dark nights work in your favour, and set aside an evening to follow our step-by-step manicure!

1) Start by removing any old nail polish. Use a cotton wool pad and soak it thoroughly with nail varnish remover. Then press it against the nail for a count of ten before you actually rub. This softens the polish and makes it easier to remove.

2) Shape your nails with an emery board, filing from the sides to the middle. Don't file down too short at the corners, as this can weaken growth.

3) Now soak nails in warm soapy water for ten minutes. You can use liquid soap or washing-up liquid for this. If your nails are really stained or dirty try using a nail brush. Scrub gently, though, and don't damage your cuticles. After soaking, dry each finger individually and use the towel to softly push back the cuticle.

4) Cuticle remover is next. Simply

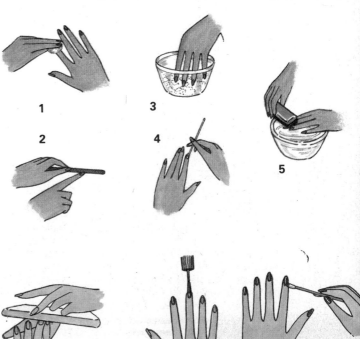

1

2

3

4

5

6

7

8

6

apply it around the cuticle and wait for 5 to 10 minutes. When the time's up, use an orange stick wrapped in cotton wool to gently lift and push back the cuticle from the nail. Be careful that you don't push too hard, you could damage the nail.

5) Now dip your fingertips back into the soapy water and gently use the nail brush to remove any bits of cuticle that are left over. Dry your hands well afterwards.

6) If you're not going to use nail polish, you might like to try buffing your nails to give them a shine. Buffing also increases blood circulation in the nail and encourages growth.

7) Applying your nail polish is next. It's best to do this in three simple strokes — one down the middle, and one on either side. Use a base coat first to prevent nail discolouration and also to give a smooth surface to work on. Now apply the colour of your choice — keeping each coat thin and smooth. 3 coats is a good guide, but you have to remember to let each one dry thoroughly before going on. A top coat or a sealer means your polish should last a day or two longer, so it is worth it. Extend it right under your nail for extra strength.

8) To give your manicure that really professional look, dip a cotton bud in nail varnish remover and lightly run it around the edge of the fingernail and cuticle to catch any spilled polish.

 **HAIR HAIR!**
Now that spring is just around the corner, let's see what we can do to get your hair in tip-top condition!

How often do you wash your hair? Every week, or every two days? It's really up to you, but a general rule is to wash your hair when it looks or feels dirty. Normal to dry hair can last out longer than greasy hair — it needs washed every second day to look good. Just sticking your head under the tap and slapping on shampoo isn't the way to achieve beautiful hair, though. Shampooing has to be done properly to work. Wet hair thoroughly with warm water. Pour a little shampoo into your palm and then rub your hands together before applying to your hair. Work it in for two or three minutes with your fingertips until you get a rich lather worked up. Now rinse thoroughly with warm water, until your hair's 'squeaky' clean! You shouldn't really need a second application of shampoo — most modern ones clean very thoroughly the first time — but if you feel you do, simply repeat the previous instructions.

Use your conditioner now — combing through for extra concentration. When you rinse it off, once again rinse two or three times, and make the last rinse one of cold or cool water to

close your pores — especially helpful if you've got very greasy hair.

Now blot your hair with a soft towel — rubbing only encourages oily secretions. Wrap the towel around your head for a few minutes until the worst of the dampness is soaked up. Use your fingers or a wide-toothed comb to style hair as this will not damage it. Never use a brush on wet hair — it causes splitting and leaves your hair in bad condition.

Don't expect to find the perfect shampoo at first go! You'll probably have to experiment with lots to discover the right one for you. Read the labels carefully — and take into account whether your hair is tinted, permed or bleached. Go for a gentle, frequent wash shampoo if you're not sure — they suit most people and won't cause any harm. Ask your hairdresser if you've any problems — he'll be only too pleased to help!

LOOK GOOD —EAT WELL!
Spring is here, and it's time to get out of your winter eating habits! Those extra few pounds may have kept you warm, but they'll just look out of place in your summer clothes. So, now's the month to make sure your diet is a healthy one — and cut out those crisps and chocs until the bulges are gone!

The key to a sound healthy diet is variety, and a balance of all the necessary ingredients — proteins, carbohydrates and fats. Proteins include meat, fish, milk, cheese and eggs, and your body needs protein to function well and for you to grow. But these foods should be eaten in moderation; because too much protein only turns to fat. Vegetables contain protein, too, but unlike animal products they have less fat. Beans, soya, cereals and pulses are all good examples of vegetable protein.

Carbohydrates are found in puddings and jams and should be reduced as much as possible in your diet. Try a sweetener in your tea or coffee instead of your usual two sugars — it tastes the same anyway and does you more good!

Complex carbohydrates are found in fruits, vegetables, grains and pulses and are good for you. They produce energy and the fibre necessary to keep your digestion system working regularly. In fact, complex carbohydrates should make up 70-80% of your daily food intake.

Fats can be found in vegetable oils, chicken, turkey, nuts, butter, ice-cream and milk, and give you energy and help to structure body tissues. But you only need a very small amount each day. They just do harm if taken in excess over a long time.

Now that you know what your body needs, it's a case of working out a diet you like and sticking to it. And remember that no matter what you eat, you won't burn up those calories unless you exercise in some way. The more active you are, the quicker you're likely to get back into shape!

Continued on page 14

what's *love* got to do with it?

It has recently come to the notice of the Patches office that a growing number of people are indulging in a rather disgusting pastime called — kissing!

We went out and about on the streets of Britain to catch the filthy culprits and ask them why they do it. We also asked a few innocent passers-by for their views on the subject.

PETER
My first kiss was very short, because I didn't find it very interesting — and it was probably my worst kiss, too. As for who I'd most like to kiss, I'll have to be really boring and say Madonna!

AUDREY
I was really disappointed in my first kiss — it wasn't nearly as good as I'd been told it would be. I'd like to kiss Robert Smith of The Cure. By the way, Peter isn't my boyfriend!

WAYNE
I can't remember my first kiss at all, but my worst one was probably from my mum when I was wee. I'm training to be a chartered accountant and I'd like to kiss this woman who works in the Abbey National — I'm taking some letters to her now.

COLIN
I'm not going to kiss Susan — my girlfriend'd kill me!
My first kiss was from my first girlfriend and it was great. My worst kiss was probably one from my dog — all wet and slobbery. I'd like to kiss Bo Derek.

SUSAN
My first kiss was OK, but I had a horrible one once from a boy at school — he nearly swallowed me! I'd like to kiss Morrissey.

IAN
My first kiss happened when I was about nine and it was from a girl who lived in Wormit — that's in Fife.
I wouldn't say no to a kiss from Victoria Principal.

FIONA
My first kiss was from a boyfriend in Primary seven. It was a bit slobbery.
It's a bit embarrassing banging people's teeth when you kiss them, isn't it? I'd like to kiss Roddy Frame from Aztec Camera.

ANONYMOUS
My first kiss was really boring — not as exciting as I expected, anyway. My worst kiss was from this girl who screwed up her eyes and wouldn't move her lips.
I got a few horrible kisses at Christmas, too. I hate that, 'cos all your old relatives kiss you — even the blokes! I'd really like to kiss Madonna — I think she's beautiful. By the way, this is my dog, Rio — she's twelve weeks old.

PETER AND AUDREY, both 17

WAYNE, 17 going on 18

IAN AND FIONA, both 15

Disgusting, isn't it — all these people wanting to kiss each other? And it's not just ordinary mortals who're at it, either. It seems that the rich and famous are latching on to this, too.

Limahl (who?) and friend.

Marilyn and his mum!

Steve Norman and some girl. Think she's a Page 3 model or something . . .

COLIN AND SUSAN, both 18

ANONYMOUS, 17

Even our very own Prime Minister — a woman who should know better! Makes you ashamed to be British, doesn't it?

If you're one of the guilty parties, here's a few facts guaranteed to put you off kissing for ever.

● An American couple had to be separated by firemen after their braces locked together during a passionate embrace.

● Every time you kiss, such a strain is put on your heart that your life is shortened by five minutes.

● Glandular fever is known as the 'kissing disease' because that's how it's passed on.

Now that you've decided to have nothing at all to do with this revolting habit, here's how to make sure the boys stay away from you.

do

Eat lots of curries or garlic bread before you go out on a date. Not only do they make your breath stink, the smell oozes from your pores, too.

Forget to brush your teeth. Bits of steak trapped between your teeth are sure to put him off.

Use a really disgusting shade of lipstick and slap it on any old how. A few bits of lipstick on your front teeth add the finishing touch.

don't

Use lipsalve — it'll only keep your lips soft, moist and very tempting.

Go to the dentist. He'll give you fillings, polish your teeth and just generally make them look good. A mouthful of dirty, rotten teeth and bleeding gums is much more off-putting.

Re-apply your lipstick as the evening goes on. Let it smudge on glasses and 'bleed' over the edge of your lips.

So there you are — 6 pieces of advice to make sure you're safe from kissing.

Of course, if you're one of the weirdos who actually *enjoy* kissing just do the exact opposite!

DIARY OF A VAMPIRE

OR EXCUSE ME, BUT YOUR NECK IS IN MY TEETH!

Diary Of A Vampire was an overwhelming success in the weekly Patches. So here, by popular demand, Draconia returns . . . on holiday!

> **SPECIALLY WRITTEN FOR PATCHES BY CAROLYN JONES**

Mr & Mrs Jones,
666 Horror Close,
Chapel House,
Newcastle.

Dear Mummy and Daddy,
Am having a wonderful time! Have made friends with a boy called Danny. He is very nice! The Lights and Pleasure Beach are great! Lynne's mum lets us do what we want, so we stay out nearly all night at discos, the Pleasure Beach etc., etc.
See you soon,
Love,
Draconia.
P.S. How is Beat?

Johnny Jackson,
11 Death Drive,
Chapel House,
Newcastle.

My Dearest Darling,
Sweetheart Johnny, Blackpool is very boring without you here. I miss you dreadfully and haven't looked at another boy. I can't wait to get home so I can see you again.
Lots of love,
Draconia.
xxxxxxxxxxxx
P.S. I love U!!

Count Dracula,
Dracula's Castle,
Transylvania.

Dear Uncle Drac,
(In case you've woken up!) I'm in Blackpool with Lynne and her mum and dad. It's great! Dead romantic. When can I come back to Transylvania?
Love, your (fave) niece,
Draconia.
P.S. Say Hi to Frank for me!

> Now what *really* happened in Blackpool.

SATURDAY NIGHT/ SUNDAY MORNING

Me and Lynne had a disco in the coach on the way up, it was great except for the fact it was too cramped to do Agadoo properly.

The driver was a maniac who kept swerving across the road then screaming at me and Lynne. You'd have thought we were distracting him or something!

We arrived at our hotel at about 4 p.m. Our room was dead nice. Two single beds, two small wardrobes and a chest of drawers.

Unpacked, got changed, then me and Lynne went to the Pleasure Beach. However, I threw up on the horses so we went to see what the local neck talent was like!

We arrived back at the hotel between 2 and 4 o'clock in the morning and went straight to sleep! But it's just not the same as a comfy coffin.

SUNDAY AFTERNOON

1.00 p.m. Already Lynne has covered all the walls of the hotel room with Wham posters!

1.30 p.m. I have discovered that I have only £5 of my spending money left. Where on earth did £65 go?

I told Lynne and she snarled that there was no way I was going to scrounge off her. Some friend. She could at least have slipped me a tenner.

Lynne wanted to go to the tower and I was dragged along. However, I didn't go in with her because I wanted to save my cash. I was standing outside waiting for her, admiring all the holiday-makers pushing their way in (it looked a bit like kids getting on the school buses but not as violent) when this lad came up and offered to pay me in.

If he thought *I* was the sort of girl to accept money off a perfect stranger, then he was right. Boys can be so gullible. I got him to pay me in, then left him! I found Lynne in the Undersea World talking to a fish. Later on that boy caught up and demanded to know why I'd disappeared. He had an evil glint in his eyes, so I lied that I hadn't meant to, I just got lost in the crowd. He was stupid enough to believe me.

Lynne nudged me and asked who he was and he introduced himself as Rick. We then had to put up with him tagging along with us for the rest of the afternoon. He said he'd come and pick me up at my hotel that night. I told him to bring one of his friends with him for Lynne.

Lynne started to protest about it when we got back to the hotel, saying it wasn't fair on H___s etc., so I explained to her that it was one way of getting [a] free meal ticket. That shut her up!

Anyway, at 7 o'clock, Dick or Mick or whatever and his friend were standing outside the hotel. Close up, his friend was absolutely *gorgeous*. He has light brown hair, dark brown eyes, and when he smiles, dimples! I could hardly take my eyes off him. Nor his name. It was love at first — sorry, sight! Nick or Vick or whatever looked a bit dis-chuffed, especially when he made a pass at Lynne and she dropped an ice-cream down his neck! Gorgeous is called Danny, and he is a wonderful kisser!

MONDAY

Lynne, me, Danny and Sick, or Vick or whatever, went to Madame Tussauds. It was quite good, although I was very disappointed with the Horror Chamber. My uncle Dracula does not look anything as ugly as that. It is an insult to the family. That means me as well!

After that we went to the Pleasure Beach and I got my photo taken with a cardboard George Michael. How I wish it had been the *real* George Michael! Then he went on the Logs. Wick or Nick or whatever his name is got soaked. Ha, ha, ha! I'd realised he was a bit of a wet but not quite such a big drip!

Then me and Lynne went back to the hotel for our tea and the boys said they'd take us to a disco afterwards. We spent about two hours getting ourselves tarted up and fighting over each other's clothes.

The disco was absolutely brilliant. Especially when Lynne spilt cider down Tick or Kick or whatever's Le Breve top. Ha, ha, ha! He was going to throw one over Lynne, but we restrained him.

After that we went for a walk along the promenade for about an hour (that boy, whatever his name is, moaned constantly), then we went for a ride on a tram which was covered in light bulbs, after which we were fit to crash out.

TUESDAY

Probably the worst thing about waking up in the wrong hotel room is the sinking feeling in the pit of your stomach when you know something's not quite right and it's only very gradually that the truth begins to dawn.

In this case, the thing that wasn't quite right was the fact that I was in a double bed and Lynne was in a single bed between a large wardrobe and a television.

The wrong room was embarrassing enough!! When we arrived back at *our* hotel we got an hour-long lecture off Lynne's mum and dad about staying out all night!

After lunch, Danny and Nick or Thick or whatever, came to call for us so we went to the zoo. It was really good, especially at feeding time. We then went to Splash Land.

I am falling more and more in love with Danny. Every time I look at him it makes me feel like I've just been plugged in as one of the illuminations!

While we were having our tea Lynne's mum and dad calmly announced that, as we hadn't come back to the hotel last night, we had to go to a night club with them!

We were in bed by 11.45 p.m. Huh!

WEDNESDAY

I had a brilliant dream about Danny last night. Lynne says I was talking in my sleep, but will not tell me what I was saying. How embarrassing!

It rained all day so when the boys came to call for us we went to the tower. However the entire population of Blackpool had the same idea and it was absolutely jam-packed, so we left and went back to Danny's hotel room to play cards. I lost — but only because I kept getting bad hands!

I also sent my postcards. They cost me 20p as well — excluding the stamps. *They* came to 68p!

After tea we went to the disco. It was great!

THURSDAY

As our holiday is drawing to an end we decided to paint the town red. So we went on everything at the Pleasure Beach about six times. I also brought my dinner up about six times, but I won't go into detail about that.

After tea we decided to give the disco a miss and we spent all night travelling up and down on the trams and looking at the lights.

Danny wants us to write to each other when we go home, but I am not sure if I want to. Mick or Vick or whatever at last plucked up the courage to ask Lynne out. She collapsed laughing, so he stormed off! Ha, ha, ha!

FRIDAY

The last day of our hols.! I tried to keep a stiff upper lip when I met Danny, but I couldn't and burst out crying into my hamburger! In a crowded café as well. I don't blame Zick, or Yick, or whatever, for walking off!

Me and Danny spent our last night together walking across the beach (until the tide came in — then we went on to the promenade).

Oh, life is so cruel!

BEST OF ENE

Nick and I hated each other, everyone knew that, but now I wasn't so sure . . .

I ALMOST missed the entire trip.

"Kim! Your passport!" screamed my mum as I tumbled up the road, late anyway and dragging this hold-all that felt like it was full of stone knickers.

"What kept you?" Moira moaned, her head half-way out of the coach window. "Miss Henshaw's had another nervous breakdown thinking we'll miss the plane because of you."

"Sorry. The cat was sick in my ski-hat . . . among other things." I scrambled up the steps and fell heavily on to the feet of a boy on the front seat as the coach jerked forward. Not just any boy, of course — oh no. It had to be Nick Carter — old superstar himself.

We glared at each other before I tottered away to the back seat, looking as poised as anybody with a runny nose and hair like an exploded haystack could manage.

"What are you all worked up about?" Moira asked as I collapsed, red-faced beside her. "You only fell. You couldn't help it."

"You know what Nick's like," I muttered. "He'll be making digs about me falling for him."

She giggled. "Well, let's face it. Everybody does."

"Not everybody. Not me! I'm not a member of the Nick Carter Fan Club, thank you!"

"OK, OK. Don't jump down my throat. He's not my type either — not like Dave." Dave is this guy she's been going out with since they were in nappies. "But you've got to admit he's very attractive."

She'd said that last Tuesday lunchtime as well, when we were watching the team's football practice and Nick had raced towards us doing a lot of fancy footwork.

"He's got terrific legs," she'd sighed.

"So has a centipede," I snapped back, "and more of them!"

The trouble was that everybody in our school knew me and Nick Carter hated each other and had done for years. I was always putting him down for being conceited and he reckoned I was a loud-mouthed lunatic. We couldn't meet without quarrelling.

"They say he's a fantastic skier too," Moira said, dreamily.

"It's a good thing Dave's coming with us on this holiday," I said. "You're beginning to sound like the rest of this lot."

She laughed and we began to talk about what a great time we planned to have in Austria. We'd never been abroad before and it had taken us ages to save up but we were sure it would be worth it.

And then, for me, there was the fact that I would be under the same roof as Nick for a whole week. How would I cope? Hide from everyone that I was crazy about a boy I was supposed to loathe?

"Excuse me," said a voice, "but I think this is your earring. I think maybe you dropped it when you got on this morning." He grinned. It was Chris Holroyd, a friendly boy who'd only been around since Christmas so I didn't know him very well.

"Oh, thanks, Chris." I took the earring from him.

"Do you mind if I join you?" he asked.

"Yeah, sure," I replied, moving my anorak to make room.

* * * *

"Chris Holroyd fancies you like mad." It was already Day Four of the holiday and we were in our bedroom taking off anoraks and boots after an exhausting day of trying to stay upright at ninety miles an hour downhill. I examined a big purple bruise on my left shin.

"Did he tell you that?"

"He doesn't need to. It's obvious." Moira smiled as she rubbed her feet with a towel. "He never takes his eyes off you. And I don't think he should even be in our group. I'm sure he's not a beginner."

"You mean he can ski — properly?"

"I mean he's pretending he can't. He keeps joking with Helmut about something and when Helmut's teaching us Chris isn't listening."

"He speaks good German," I agreed, "and he hasn't fallen flat on his face yet. Apart from that I think you're crazy."

"You just don't want to admit it. Come on, Kim, stop fooling about. What's the problem?"

I took off one sock, very slowly.

"There's no problem! I like Chris. He's nice."

"Nice! Is that all, just nice? I don't understand you. You've been in a weird mood all week. I mean, last night for instance, we were all having a really good laugh and you hardly said a word. Except when you were needling Nick Carter, of course."

"No, I wasn't. I didn't . . ." I said quickly.

She didn't reply for a minute. She was watching me looking at my foot.

"Perhaps I'm being a bit thick. Perhaps this slagging-off Nick routine is all a big cover-up. Perhaps it's him you're keen on."

"Don't be stupid! Of course I'm not!" I began to massage my foot furiously.

"Oh? Because I'll tell you something else. From the way he looks at you when he thinks no-one's noticing, I'd say he was pretty interested himself. So just who is fooling who, I wonder?"

"I thought you were going for a shower?"

Moira picked up her towel. "I am." At the door she turned. "So go on — if you can't stand Nick and you don't fancy Chris — who does turn you on?"

"Howard Jones," I grinned. "I'm saving myself for Howard. Hey, Moira, when you get frostbite does it begin with your toes going numb?"

"Yes. Then they go black and drop off one by one!" She slammmed out.

* * * *

Slowly I began to pick through my clothes for something to wear. I didn't need Moira to tell me about Chris. I knew.

I pulled a bright pink sweater over my head and gazed in the mirror. "What an idiot," I told the pale-faced image staring back. "What a messy, stupid situation. Suppose she's right. Suppose Nick . . . no, don't. Moira's always imagining things. What did he say last night . . ? 'Your conversation, Kim, is about as interesting as watching grass grow.' Huh!"

The door flew open and Moira bounced in, pink and turbanned from her shower.

"Sorry I blew," she said. "It's none of my business is it? It's just I don't like to see you looking so miserable."

"That's OK," I said, forcing a smile. "You're probably right — about Chris, I mean. Thanks for putting me in the picture."

"You mean you . . ?"

"I don't mean anything, Moira. Let's just leave it for a bit. Maybe we'll get together. I don't know."

I didn't think I'd slept at all that night but I must have, because all of a sudden it was morning and Moira was shrieking Happy Birthday! down my ear.

Mum had put a few little presents and cards in my case so I had those as well, but otherwise it was a non-event. Just another day. "You won't mind being away for your birthday?" Mum had said.

"No, of course not. It's not like when you're a kid, is it?" I'd said. But after we'd eaten at night I got this sudden wave of homesickness.

I wanted to be back, with everybody making a big fuss and Mum bringing in the cake with candles and everything . . . Tears welled up and I had to dash out quickly before anyone noticed. I made for the lift.

"Kim!" I turned. It was Chris. "Wait."

MIES

"No, Chris. I'm alright, but I want to go upstairs for a bit. Please."

He grabbed my arm. "Hang on. We've got a surprise. Close your eyes and come with me."

I let him guide me a few steps and then I opened my eyes.

"Surprise! Surprise!" they all yelled. "Happy birthday!"

Everyone was gathered in the bar and there was a glittering heap of little presents on the table and Klaus, the head-waiter, was coming in with a huge cake covered with burning candles. "Come on, Kim, blow them out. Make a wish!"

And I did and they all sang Happy Birthday so I cried like a two-year-old and laughed at the same time. It was lovely.

"Aren't you pleased?" whispered Moira. "It was Chris who thought of the cake. He asked the chef to make it and I made everybody keep it secret."

"It's magic," I said, hugging her. "You're all very kind."

*   *   *   *

And then I was with Nick. I don't know how it happened but suddenly it seemed as if there was just the two of us, talking together, and everything else was a blur in the background. The people and the music faded and I was only aware of him and his eyes were warm and laughing. Maybe I said things that amused him but I don't remember what they were. It could have been minutes or hours but in that time I knew I'd given myself away, shown him how I felt. It was in my face and in my voice and he knew . . .

Then the dizziness came again and, this time, it wasn't from happiness.

"Oh, I feel awful." My head was bursting and I felt sick. "Moira . . ?"

"Come on. You need the bathroom."

She gave me a glass of water and some aspirin and pushed me under the duvet. I slid into a confused sleep and woke with a thundering headache.

"Hey, Moira," I whispered as a lazer beam of Alpine sun drilled into my skull. "What happened to my party?"

"It was rocking — till the birthday girl crashed out. Somebody played a very nasty practical joke and spiked your Coke with vodka. I got him to admit it in the end."

"Who? Why?"

"You know why, surely? Nick, of course. You've always said he was a pain in the neck. Well, you're right. Dead childish . . ."

She went raving on but I wasn't listening. I turned away and the tears poured down my face. There was no question of my going ski-ing. I couldn't possibly. I lay there all morning wishing I were dead and wondering why he'd been so mean.

By lunchtime I managed to stagger out for some air. It smelt lovely. Frost and pine needles. I crunched off through the snow towards the cafe. Hot chocolate would be a good move right now, I thought.

I was into my third cup when Moira and Dave and the others came in.

"Glad to see you can move all the bits and pieces again," Dave said, cheerfully. "We've come to watch Nick Carter's mob do the Black Run. Somebody's challenged the arch-villain to a race, and all the advanced group are doing it. Should be great."

"Except he'll probably win!" Moira snapped, looking loyally at me. I buried my nose in chocolate foam and fixed my attention on the skiers.

They sped like tiny missiles down the curling white snake of the run, nearer and nearer, until two shot ahead of the main bunch.

"There's Nick! I told you so," Dave shouted. "There, in red. I don't know who's with him but he looks good."

He looks better, I thought, and I can easily guess who it is. As we watched, the green-clad figure shot past Nick and reached the flag with seconds to spare. They were too far away for us to see their expressions but we saw Nick walk over and congratulate Chris in the midst of the clapping spectators. Chris nodded and turned away immediately. Even from that distance you could see the utter contempt in the gesture.

"I reckon Chris did that deliberately to show him what he thinks of him," muttered Moira. "Good for him. Aren't you pleased?"

I just smiled sadly and said nothing.

"Kim." It was Nick. Pale under his tan. Sick at losing, no doubt.

"I'm sorry about last night. It was a really stupid thing to do and I don't know why . . . anyway I'm sorry you were ill. I didn't intend that, honestly."

"Oh, it's OK," I said, studying the rim of my cup carefully.

"I spoilt your party. Moira's chewed my ears off about it and I suppose you saw Chris burn me off in the race just now? It's your turn now. Go on. I deserve it."

I shook my head.

Abruptly he sat down. "What's the matter with us, Kim?"

"What do you mean?" I wouldn't look at him.

He sighed. "All the aggro between us. It seems like we've hated each other for ever, but, last night, well, maybe I'm wrong but I felt you'd changed. I'd fixed your drink by the time I got the message . . ."

"Was it to get back at me for needling you?"

"Yeah, sort of. There was Chris too. He's never let you alone all week. It was really getting to me."

Then I looked up. His face was dark and troubled and he reached for my hand.

"Listen, I'm fed-up with playing games with you. You can laugh if you want to and everybody else will fall about, but I don't care. Just tell me. Is it Chris or . . ?"

I swallowed hard. Oh, this was going to take a lot of living down. He was right. They'd all have a good laugh, remind us of all the insults and quarrels, and Moira would tell me a million times over how much nicer Chris was . . . as if I cared . . .

"Chris," I said, leaning close and bringing my mouth near to his, "is just a friend."

Continued from page 7

TAKE STOCK!

It's spring cleaning time, and that means digging out your tatty make-up bag and its contents. Lay everything out and ask yourself a few vital questions. Are the brushes and sponges clean? Are you carrying around a lipstick you haven't used for six months? Is your favourite eye pencil blunt? If you're anything like the Patches gang we'll bet you're embarrassed to even admit that make-up bag is yours!

Let's start with the bag itself. Would a wash make it look like new? No, well, throw it out and treat yourself to a new one! They're not expensive.

Now for your make-up brushes. Fill a bowl with a dash of washing-up liquid and warm water and dip each brush in it individually. Squeeze each brush gently until it's clean. Then rinse the brush thoroughly and dry with a tissue.

Cosmetic sponges, sponge applicators and powder puffs are next. Once again soapy water is your best bet, but you may find that you have to change the water quite a lot for this — sponges hold more than brushes, you see. Rinse the sponges under running water and then squeeze dry. Leave them to dry naturally and they should be as good as new the next day!

Now take a good look at the tubes and containers your make-up is in. Give lipsticks a wipe with a damp cloth to catch any colour that may have strayed. Use a cotton bud to get to awkward corners and wipe any mirrors clean.

Check that your eye pencils and lip pencils are sharp enough to do their job properly. If they're not, sharpen them with a special eye pencil sharpener.

Before you replace all your spotlessly clean make-up in your bag, be ruthless and stop carrying around the things you don't need or use. There's no point building up muscles lugging around half of Boots, is there?

BE A SMOOTHIE!

Summer's here! This month it's time to think ahead to long lazy days on the beach — or lying out in your garden. You want to make the most of all that sunshine, and a tan looks best on smooth legs!

How do you get rid of unwanted hair? Shaving is the quickest way, but it also leaves a horrible stubble and has to be done every two or three days.

If you prefer to shave — use a ladies' razor with a new blade. Lather up your legs with soap and water before you start, and try to keep the razor going in a continuous movement. Never use a razor on dry legs — that's just asking for nicks and cuts!

An electric ladyshaver is a good idea — it makes shaving painless and easy if you're a beginner at this business!

Depilatory creams, like Immac, Nair and Veet , actually dissolve the hair shaft so that the hair doesn't grow back for a week or two — perfect for holidays!

Read the instructions on your depilatory cream very carefully and remember to do the patch test if it's the first time you've used it. You could turn out to be allergic to it. Don't use it on broken or spotty skin, either.

If you've got a bit of money to spare, you might think about waxing. It's a great idea if you want to get rid of the hair for four weeks or more and, because the hair is pulled out from the root, the regrowth is slow and fine. You can wax your own legs at home with a kit from the chemist — Wax A Way or Louis Marcel's Strip Wax — but you'd be better to go to a professional beauty salon the first time, just so that you can see exactly how it's done.

Bleaching might be the answer if your hair is very fine. You can buy a special bleaching preparation at the chemist, and you should do a skin patch test first. Bleaching makes the hair so light that it's hardly noticeable, so it is an idea if you don't fancy any of the other methods!

Electrolysis is the only permanent way to get rid of unwanted hair, but it is very expensive and has to be done by an expert. Ask your hairdresser or beauty salon if you're interested.

TOE THE LINE!

Feet have to look good for summer — when did you last treat yourself to a pedicure? Here's how to go about it:

1) Clip your toe nails straight across using nail clippers, not scissors.

2) File the nails smooth.

3) Soak your feet in soapy water and give them a good scrub with a nail brush.

4) Use a pumice stone to attack any dry or calloused areas

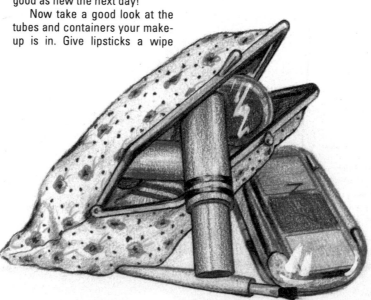

BEAUTY

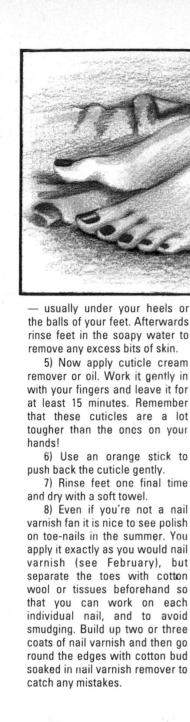

Continued on page 86

— wash in, spray in, mousse — but they'll only last until your next shampoo, so they're great if you're not quite sure about the change! Temporary colours (Shaders and Toners, Crazy Colour) cost under £1, but don't expect to go blonde overnight — they can't lighten your hair because they don't contain bleach.

Semi-permanent hair colours (Glints, Harmony) last for 3 or 4 shampoos. They're stronger than the temporary rinses, but once again don't promise to make your hair colour any lighter.

Permanent hair colourants are exactly that — permanent! So don't mess about with this type of hair colourant unless it's being done by a professional hairdresser — especially the first time. Your hairdresser could suggest all kinds of hair colouring tricks you might like — highlighting, touch colouring — there are loads for you to choose from.

So, if you want to brighten up your life — follow our advice and go colour crazy. It's so simple and easy you'll wonder why you didn't think of it before!

— usually under your heels or the balls of your feet. Afterwards rinse feet in the soapy water to remove any excess bits of skin.

5) Now apply cuticle cream remover or oil. Work it gently in with your fingers and leave it for at least 15 minutes. Remember that these cuticles are a lot tougher than the ones on your hands!

6) Use an orange stick to push back the cuticle gently.

7) Rinse feet one final time and dry with a soft towel.

8) Even if you're not a nail varnish fan it is nice to see polish on toe-nails in the summer. You apply it exactly as you would nail varnish (see February), but separate the toes with cotton wool or tissues beforehand so that you can work on each individual nail, and to avoid smudging. Build up two or three coats of nail varnish and then go round the edges with cotton bud soaked in nail varnish remover to catch any mistakes.

eyes, you can make them look electric by having blonde highlights!

Skin tones are important, too. Pale skin looks best with darker shades of hair, whereas red hair makes a sallow complexion look good. If you're naturally pink, choose a brown shade as it's most flattering.

You can change the colour of your hair yourself at home if you want. There are three main kinds of hair colourants — and they're all available at your chemist and hairdresser. Temporary colourants come in many forms

COLOURWISE!

If you'd like to change the colour of your hair you have to take into consideration the colour of your eyes and skin tone, too. Brown eyes tend to be lost with brown hair, but show up much more dramatically with red or gold highlights in the hair.

Green eyes which need extra emphasis can be lifted with a red rinse or highlights, but fair hair works equally well here too. If you've light brown hair and blue

15

Starfile

Name: GEORGE MICHAEL

Date of Birth: 25/6/63

Height: 6 FT

Previous Jobs: WASHER-USHER

Viewing Habits: TOP OF THE POPS

Fave Record: 'LOVE MACHINE' BY THE MIRACLES

Tastebud Temptations: MAYONNAISE. I LOVE IT ON CHIPS, BREAD AND MOST OF ALL, ON PRAWNS!!

Favourite Person: ME

First Date: SORRY, CAN'T REMEMBER!

Most Exciting Place You've Ever Been: NEW YORK

Earliest Musical Memory: WHEN I WAS SEVEN, I WAS GIVEN A CASSETTE RECORDER FOR MY BIRTHDAY. I USED TO RECORD POP SONGS FROM THE RADIO WITH IT.

How Long Do You Sleep Each Night? ABOUT FIVE HOURS, USUALLY.

Likes: DANCING, PERFORMING, NITECLUBBING.

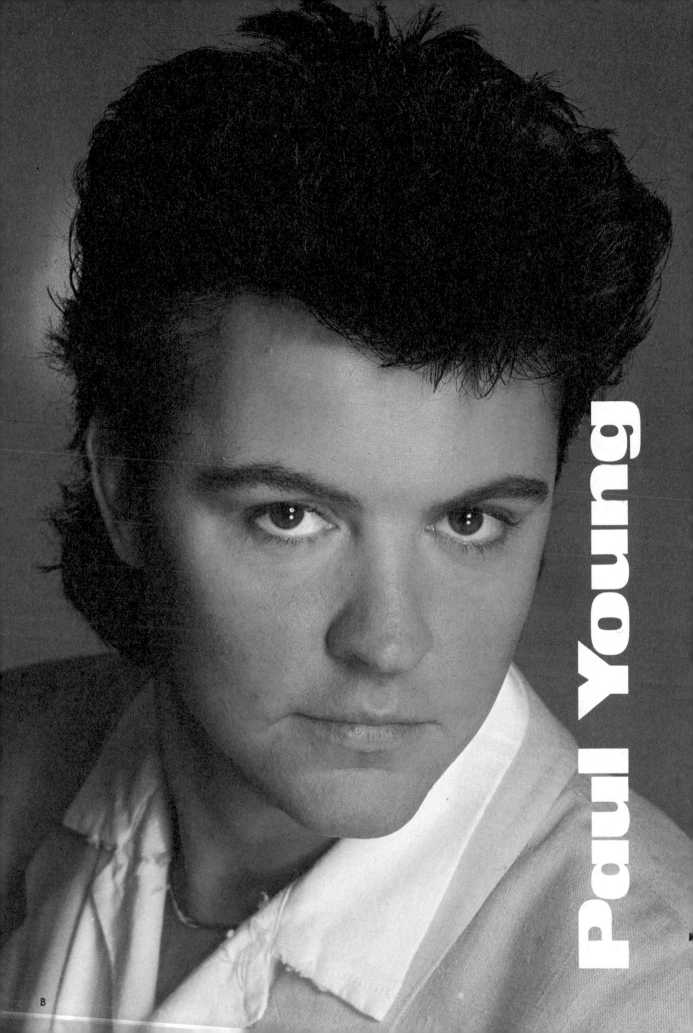

Paul Young

Now Get Out Of That!

Patches present 10 ways to get out of some classic dodgy situations . . .

● You've just walked into the living-room and caught your big brother getting stuck into his girlfriend.

Grab a trayful of crisps and shout "Crisps! Popcorn! Ices!", pretending to be an usherette. Then shine a torch on their faces, shouting at the top of your voice, "Enough of that in the back row please, ladies and gents!"

● You're in a posh restaurant when the waiter plonks down the weirdest-looking thing in front of you and you haven't a clue how to eat it!

Just claim with a grin that, "The last time I was out to dinner with George Michael he said the only way to enjoy this dish is to take it up in your hands and bite it!"

Oh — and try not to dribble!

● You bump into the head teacher at the school gates — half an hour after school started.

First thing to do is ruffle up the old uniform a bit and breathe heavily as though you've been hurrying to get to school. "Oh thank goodness I bumped into you, sir, it'll save me coming to your office. It's my pet hamster you see — did I tell you? Well it's not been very well . . ."

Just carry on like this for at least fifteen minutes, by which time any self-respecting adult will have either been reduced to tears or a deep sleep. Either way he'll certainly have forgotten you were half an hour late for school.

● You're out with the punkiest guy in town, when you bump into Great Aunt Florence in the street.

Easiest way is just to take the boy and shove him into the nearest pram — making sure you get rid of the baby first — drop a few coins in a hat and shout, "Penny For The Guy".

Don't worry if it's not Halloween, though, you could always try and convince Aunt Florence he's the latest line in life-size Cabbage Patch dolls.

● Amorous Andy's got you down a back alley and is about to try the ol' 'wandering hands' trick!

Apart from stilleto-ing him where it hurts, just tell him his hair's out of place and his medallion's squint. While he spends half an hour adjusting these, you nip away!

● You're caught by your trendiest chum while you're in your bedroom sniffing away tearfully to the latest 'Des O'Connor Sings Sad Songs' elpee!

One way to get out of this is just to claim you were crying because it was so bad — but then again she'd probably think you were so untrendy to listen to it in the first place.

The other alternative is to say you were smashing it to bits when one of the bits got in your eye, making it water.

● You're stopped in the street by some worthy person collecting money for charity — when you've only got your 15p bus fare left to your name.

The most obvious way out is just to walk past and pretend you never noticed them. This is rather difficult most of the time as these charitable beings tend to have their cans down your throats before you can say, "Sorry I've run completely out of change."

Then again you could always pretend to be Scottish, 'cos we know what they're like! (Watch out — Mac Ed!)

● You're two-timing your boyfriend and are just about to get torn into your new man when he walks round the corner . . .

Don't move — you're bound to look guilty. Just give him a peck on the cheek and turn to your boyfriend asking, "Oh darling, have you met my cousin Jim! We're just so close in our family you wouldn't believe it. There was I walking along the street when Jim grabbed hold of me and gave me a kiss. It's a good job you're such a loving, understanding chap, isn't it?"

Get the idea? Now just start laying on the compliments and before you know it, him and cousin Jim will be best mates!

going to a go-go!

One of the biggest rock events of 1985 was the Tube's EUROPE A GO-GO special, which was seen by over 400 million people. Patches took a peek behind the scenes.

1

2

going to a go-go

5

1. Holly 'n' the boys run through "War" as a Tyne-Tees cameraman tries to figure out whether Mark O'Toole does actually have a good side.

2. Frankie had decided to record their live performance for the soundtrack of a video they were making for American TV. So just outside "The Tube" studio was a 48-track recording studio fitted into a van!

3. "D'ya mind not touching my knobs, please?"

4. It's teatime, and as everyone piles out to the canteen, one of Frankie's road crew threatens to shoot anyone who tries to touch the band's equipment!

5. An hour later, everyone piles *out* of the canteen!
This pic of Paula Yates should teach you that if you stay in the Tube canteen *too* long, you'll probably end up giving yourself a skinhead and wearing your pyjamas on TV.

6. In come the punters! A few of "The Tube" regulars line up for the Patches camera. One of them is actually a *guy*! Which one, though? That's the question.

7. "Watch out! If my boyfriend spots me with you in the Patches annual, he'll kill me . . ."

8. The Immaculate Fools' keyboards player tries *not* to look nervous.

9. "The Tube" cameramen discover that one of the band is wearing really interesting baseball boots. Compulsive viewing, eh?

10. Jools Holland, working overtime as a bouncer, tries to hustle a real heavy lookin' guy out of the way!

11. Jools Holland, now working as a presenter, tries to persuade the rabble to scream "AAAARRRRGGGGHHH!!!" at the same time!

12. Mike Peters of The Alarm tries to scream away his spare tyre in front of 400 million people . . .

13. Finally, Frankie take the stage and Holly contemplates inviting the Patches photographer to the backstage party . . .

9

10

11

go

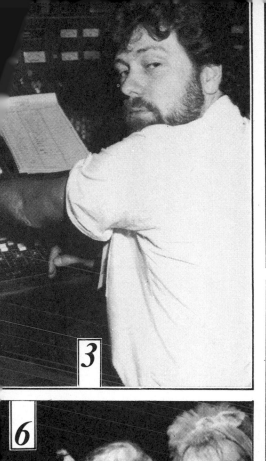

3

4

6

7

.yo

8

YAMHA DX7

12

13

Lip Tricks!

Do yours look good enough to kiss?

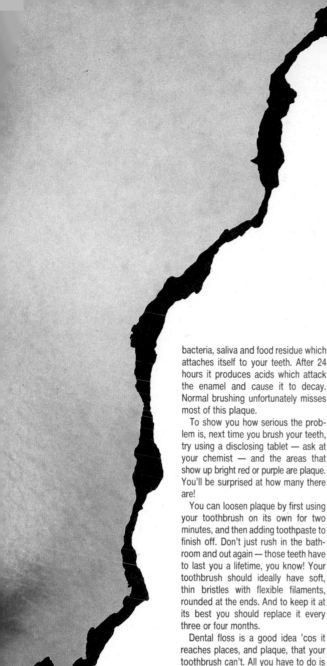

need colour, shine and careful shaping to look good. That means learning how to use a lipbrush or a lip pencil to outline your lips. This isn't at all complicated and gives a much neater, more professional look, so it is worth it. Rest your elbow on a table to help keep your hand steady if you find it difficult at first.

Outline your bottom lip first, working from the centre to one corner and then the other. Repeat on the top lip, but take extra care here to follow the natural line — you don't want to end up with points instead of curves! Now you're all set to fill in the extra colour — do this with a lipstick if that feels easier, or with a lipbrush. If you've made a mistake and let the brush slip, don't try to correct it by wiping it straight off. Try a cotton bud with a touch of make-up remover, that way it leaves no trace.

a. You can change the shape of your mouth if you're not happy with it, but you can't perform miracles! If your lips are too big, you should try outlining them just within the natural line, using a slightly paler colour than you fill in with. Don't make the two lip colours too different, though, or it could look silly. It also helps to use a darker lipstick in the centre section of your lips and a lighter shade on the outside.

b. If your lips are too thin you should outline them just outside the natural lip line. Don't overdo this, though, or it can look very obvious. It's also a good idea to stop short at the corners, and fill in your lips with a deeper colour afterwards.

c. Uneven lips are a common problem, so it's best to know how to tackle this one, too. Use two different shades of lipstick — the darker one for the fuller lip, and the lighter one for the

thinner. Once again, don't make the colours too obviously different.

If you feel that your lipstick isn't shiny enough when you've applied it, add a touch of clear lip gloss. Again, it's best to apply this with a lipbrush, but don't take the gloss to the edges of your lips as it can run. Vaseline will give you a gloss for next to nothing if you're counting those pennies!

Lipstick can run, too, but you can prevent this by carefully preparing your lips beforehand. Apply your lipstick and then blot, dusting your lips with a light coat of translucent powder and adding another coat afterwards. Keep the colour within your natural outline for the best result.

And don't let your lips get all cracked or sore, because there's nothing you can do to disguise this, no matter how much lipstick you wear! Use a lip salve or sunbloc to prevent the worst effects of the weather. Cold sores can be treated with a lotion from your pharmacist, but you should check with your doctor if you keep getting them. He may be able to prescribe something stronger.

Choosing which colour of lipstick to wear is something that worries most of us. You don't need 101 shades of lipstick to match every outfit you possess, though! In fact, you can mix lipsticks together to create a new colour yourself. Or look for brands of make-up that sell small tester sizes of lipstick. That way you can make up your mind whether or not you like it without spending a fortune!

If you're still not sure, here's a quick colour guide.

bacteria, saliva and food residue which attaches itself to your teeth. After 24 hours it produces acids which attack the enamel and cause it to decay. Normal brushing unfortunately misses most of this plaque.

To show you how serious the problem is, next time you brush your teeth, try using a disclosing tablet — ask at your chemist — and the areas that show up bright red or purple are plaque. You'll be surprised at how many there are!

You can loosen plaque by first using your toothbrush on its own for two minutes, and then adding toothpaste to finish off. Don't just rush in the bathroom and out again — those teeth have to last you a lifetime, you know! Your toothbrush should ideally have soft, thin bristles with flexible filaments, rounded at the ends. And to keep it at its best you should replace it every three or four months.

Dental floss is a good idea 'cos it reaches places, and plaque, that your toothbrush can't. All you have to do is gently work it between each tooth. Don't grind it into your gums, though. You'll only cause sore gums and bleeding.

Dentists recommend that you have a clean and check-up every six months. This will ensure that they can catch cavities that need filling — before you feel any pain! And don't put off going to the dentist until you're in agony. Drilling and filling shouldn't hurt if your dentist uses an anaesthetic, and most of them do nowadays, thank goodness!

If you've always wanted a bright, white smile, and envied popstars who do, then think again. Did you know that having a tooth capped means grinding it down to a point, and then having a permanent crown cemented in place on top? Who needs all that?

Now that we've got your teeth sparklingly clean, let's move on to your lips. It isn't just enough to slick on a layer of lipstick every morning, you know. Lips

WHAT do you notice first about a good-looking boy? His eyes, his legs, his smile . . . ? We'll bet you went for the last one, 'cos a smile is a very important part of anyone's looks. How does *yours* measure up? Are you making the most of it?

Let's start with your pearly, white teeth. What d'you mean, they're not worth looking at? That's not right! Teeth need lots of care to look their best. And don't make the mistake of thinking that bright, white teeth are the healthiest kind, 'cos they're not. Yellowish teeth are often in much better condition.

Start taking care of your teeth by careful brushing so that you remove all possible plaque. Plaque is a mixture of

COLOUR YOU'RE WEARING	COLOUR OF LIPSTICK
BLUE	Almost any shade of pink or red. You could also get away with peachy tones.
PINK	Once again pink is the best bet. Choose a shade identical to your clothes, or one which is slightly darker or lighter.
RED	Match up the shade of red you're wearing with your lipstick. Apply lightly and add gloss if you feel it's just too bright.
GREEN	You've got a free choice here! The only colour to really avoid is red — otherwise you'll look like a Christmas tree!
YELLOW & ORANGE	Go for peaches and russet shades. Or use a gloss instead. These colours tend to be tricky.

SCHOOL SAFARI

Parents never seem to realise how hazardous going to school is. They think you just skip down the road swinging your schoolbag, sit quietly in the classroom all day and skip back home again at night.

But it's not like that, is it? So here's the Patches School Survival Guide to help get you through the day!

SCHOOL SURVIVAL KIT

Gas mask
Flask of strong, black coffee
Packet of chewing gum
Your little brother's white mouse
Powder compact full of flour
Pocket mirror
Hard safety hat
Extra large schoolbag to carry this lot in!

GOING TO SCHOOL

Right! So, fully equipped, off you go to school. But half way down the road, who do you meet but Bertha, the school bully, with her 'friends' (bullies always keep a couple of these handy). As usual, she's after your dinner money.

What do you do? Easy! The conversation should go something like this.

Her: *Give's yer dinner money!*

You: *No.* (Then, as she moves menacingly towards you.) *Now, stay away or else . . .*

Her: *Or else what?*

For maximum effect, don't say anything else. Just put your hand into your pocket, take it out again and hold it about two inches under her nose. Then, very slowly, uncurl your fingers to reveal your little brother's white mouse! You won't see Bertha (or her chums) for dust! Also, they'll never come near you again. In fact, if you do this every day, maybe she'll give you *her* dinner money!

ARRIVING AT SCHOOL AND THE FIRST LESSON

That obstacle over, you arrive at school, where the first class is athletics. Here's the second problem. No-one (and I mean *no-one*) in their right mind enjoys athletics, so before going to the changing room, lock yourself in a toilet cubicle and take out your pocket mirror and powder compact full of flour. Carefully apply a thin layer all over your face and neck to make you look pale. You could dampen your fringe with some water too, to make you look like you've been sweating feverishly.

Then, arrive in the changing room, walking slowly, your palm held to your forehead and eyes slightly closed (drama lessons come in handy here). "Oh, I don't feel well," you say. "I'm so-o-o hot." Soon, they'll have found a seat for you and the teacher will be fussing over you like a mother hen. *And* you won't have to do athletics!

THE HISTORY LESSON

Next—History. Everything's fine to start with but after about five minutes, your eyelids feel heavy and your mind drifts on to other things (like that hunk in 5B). This is where the flask of strong, black coffee comes in handy—to keep you awake.

After droning on for an hour or so, the teacher'll tell you to get your books out. Now it's the turn of the chewing gum. If you're smart you'll have been chewing away at it for five or ten minutes—and so will your friends. Now, put your books inside your desk and stick the lid down with the chewing gum. Then, you all put your hands up and say, "Please, Sir, our books are stuck in our desks. The lids won't open."

By the time the teacher's found books for you to borrow or called the janitor to open the desks the lesson will be over. Clever, eh?

TAKING MESSAGES

You can practically guarantee that, once or twice a week, one of your teachers is going to ask you to take a message to another teacher. This is probably one of the most hazardous trips you'll ever make, so if you can, bribe one of the smallest first years to do it.

If you can't, you'll need your hard hat and probably your gas mask. Both of these come in very handy when taking messages to the first year chemistry class.

When you walk in, the air will be heavy with smoke and horrible, probably poisonous, fumes. While the class around you is falling like flies, you are perfectly safe. And the hard hat will protect you from flying debris when yet another acid experiment goes wrong, shattering at least 20 test tubes!

So there you are—with just a few easy-to-buy items you can protect yourself from all the dangers of yet another day at school!

TODD CARTY

Write On!

How your handwriting can give you away . . .

Are you a bit loopy? No, we're not suggesting that you're a bit round the twist! We're speaking about your handwriting!
Have a look at something you've written lately, like your homework, or your diary. Look at it very closely. Where are the loops on the letters? Are they on the capitals? Or maybe there aren't any loops at all!

(Fig. 1) Sally Smith

The *upper zone* loops are the loops that rise above the main body of your writing . . . The loop on an l or an h, for instance! If these upper loops are exaggerated (Fig. 1), then you're the sort of person who tends to live in a dream world, always imagining George Michael or Simon le Bon's going to phone out of the blue and ask you for a date! Now, however great your dreams may be, be honest and admit that they're just not likely to happen. You're also a bit too sensitive to criticism. C'mon, admit that even *you* can be wrong!

(Fig. 2) Love Sally

When the upper loops are very small (Fig. 2), you're rather a slap-happy and careless soul! Actually you're really quite clever inside, but you're just too lazy to put your brain into action! Let the other folk rush around doing all the hard work — you just like a quiet, easy life!

(Fig. 3) Dear Sally

Or perhaps there aren't any loops in your upper zone at all! (Fig. 3). Well, this just means you're a very practical and down-to-earth type! Hard working, but not desperately ambitious for fame and fortune! And you hate taking risks of any sort. Better safe than sorry is your motto!

(Fig. 4) I'm going away

The *lower zone* loops are those that drop down below the word, such as g or y. Are you one of those people whose lower loops are so long and spidery (Fig. 4) that they get all tangled up with the next line? Then you're basically scatterbrained and untidy, and tend to get really muddled and confused with anything that requires concentration or attention to detail — like exams, unfortunately! For you, the outdoor life, and sport, are much more appealing than sitting inside writing homework essays.

(Fig. 5) going to

If the lower loops are wide and "square looking" (Fig. 5), you're much too rash and impulsive. You're always rushing out and spending all your hard-earned pocket money on a fluorescent T-shirt with "WHAM!" emblazoned across the front, when what you really needed was a nice sensible pair of shoes!

(Fig. 6) going up

No loops at all (Fig. 6) mean you're a bit moody and pessimistic. But your consolation is that you're brilliant at maths (well, you should be!) or you may possess some musical talent, so get practising!

(Fig. 7) good-bye

Rather complicated, squiggly sort of loops (Fig. 7) show you're a born worrier. Do these questions sound familiar? Does this shade of lipstick go with my dress? Shall I wear this T-shirt or these shoes? Life's nothing but a series of decisions for you!

(Fig. 8) Can I Help

Now for *Capitals!* A capital letter with an extra stroke coming from the left (Fig. 8) means you're one of those people who constantly stand in front of the mirror wondering why you were born so beautiful! Don't be so vain! It's what's inside a person that really counts. Beauty is only skin deep.

(Fig. 9) Love Sue

An extra stroke joining an upper zone loop (Fig. 9) shows you to be a bit of a clever-devil. Or at least *you* think you are! Are you always on your soap box putting the world to rights? Well, we hate to say it, but at times you can be a real bore! So learn to be a good listener for a change, and give everyone's ears a well-earned rest!

(Fig. 10) Dear Ian,

Any exaggerated loop on the left of the capital (Fig. 10) tells us you're a bit on the greedy side! There's nothing you like more than lots and lots of lovely grub, the more fattening the better, too! So c'mon, put that cream cake down and have an apple instead, or the next time you step on those bathroom scales you could be in for a shock!

Patches Patches

And finally, any flourishes and twirls on your signature imply that you're a bit of an extrovert. You're also fond of material things, good living and sometimes being a bit of a show-off — so beware! Whereas *no* loops or curly bits on your signature indicate a much more practical, calm and cautious nature! But, on the negative side, you also tend to lack confidence.
Anyway, whether you're a "loopy" or a "straight" sort, watch how you write from now on. After all, just think — that application form, that love letter, what a dead give-away! So, next time you put pen to paper . . . just think before you ink!

Short of cash for new clothes? Then haul down your mum's best curtain and turn it into a super stylish skirt!

CURTAIN UP!

FOR YOUR JAZZY SKIRT...

You will need :-

Some scissors,

A reel of cotton,

Pins

And some inch wide elastic,

And most important; a curtain!

INSTRUCTIONS

1 First make a casing... Fold the top over and machine all the way along.

2 Cut off to your required length and **3** machine your hem. ALWAYS pin before you stitch.

4 Fold material in half – RIGHT SIDES TOGETHER – and stitch your seam.

5 You will end up with a tube ... Thread your elastic through the top.

6 VOILA! The completed garment...No-one would guess it was once a curtain!

TWO LITTLE PIGS WENT TO MARKET

– clothes pigs, we mean!

We thought that Natalie and Eve needed a bit of sprucing up, but they were rather broke, so we sent them off to the local market instead, and somehow they managed to transform themselves into a pair of poseurs!

This was originally a bridesmaid's dress, but we took it in at the waist and shortened it, using another cocktail dress as a guide, and a felt-tip pen!
Dress: £2 from local market
Beads: 50p from market
Kid gloves: £2.50 from thrift shop

Eve doing her Souxsie impersonation.
Black dress: £2.50 from market

◄

Modelling is so-o-o bo-oring . . .

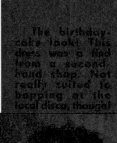

The birthday-cake look! This dress was a find from a second-hand shop. Not really suited to bopping at the local disco, though!

► Dress—local market Ski-pants— Miss Selfridge.

Natalie's leather gloves, from Dents at Selfridges, were quite expensive, but then you can afford to spend a bit on a pair of gloves when your outfit only costs £3!

"Oh no, not Cedric *again!*" Eve's blue velvet two-piece with mink collar came from a local market and didn't need any alterations. ▼

Scarlett O'Hara ▲ meets Cio Cio San!

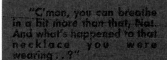

"C'mon, you can breathe in a bit more than that, Nat. And what's happened to that necklace you were wearing...?"

29

CARD

Take a good look at all the Christmas cards you get this year. Did you know you can tell someone's personality by the card they send? Read on and find out how . . .

The sender of this card is into spending money, that's why you lash out great amounts on designer cards. You're probably someone who cares about your appearance and likes to be seen as the stylish, trendy girl about town.

The bright colours also suggest that you are a bright, fun person with an outgoing personality.

Been watching Blue Peter recently? The home made Xmas card suggests that your present list is full of things made from washing-up liquid bottles and cornflake packets and that your bedroom is covered in sticky-back plastic and 'handy' double-sided sticky tape.

A home-made card shows not only that you're skint but that you put a lot of effort into things and that you really care for the person you're sending the card to.

You're one of those people who always finishes jigsaws and squeezes the very last drop out of the toothpaste tube.

The religious card suggests that, unless you pinched it outa your mum's box, you're a very traditional, upstanding person.

You're probably quite academic and would perhaps send a card like this to your teacher—after all, your taste in cards shows that you've a lot of respect for people in a position like that. In fact, at a wild guess we could say that people who send cards like this will end up as teachers and bank clerks, etc.

Definitely one for the practical, (dare we suggest boring?) card sender.

TRICKS!

This particular card shows that you're more than likely to be the outdoor type who enjoys nothing better than a romp through the snow on a winter's day.

Give the person who sent this card a pair of green wellies and they'll be in seventh heaven. You won't be able to hold them back on Xmas morning as they'll be out in the woods breathing in that fresh air.

Also the 'Edwardian Scene' suggests that you like an old-fashioned traditional Xmas—no frozen turkey for you.

Ahhh—now who's an old romantic then? And we'll bet you're an animal lover!

The person who sent this card is likely to have a house full of hamsters and white mice, and have pictures of cute little animals stuck all over their walls.

You'll probably be sending your boyfriend a little furry toy this Xmas, with a cute little message like "I Luv Ya" or something equally original, stamped on its T-shirt.

We can just see you reading bedtime stories to your nephew and nieces, then settling down with a cup of hot chocolate in front of the fire, reading the "Adventures of Harriet Hamster".

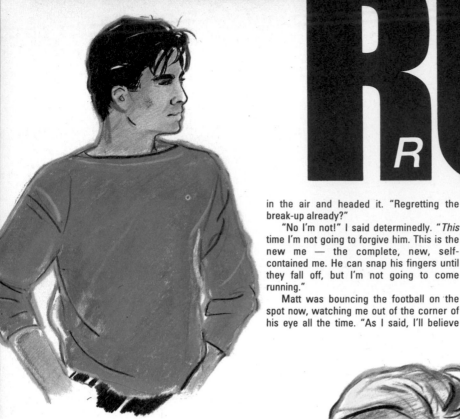

RUN

in the air and headed it. "Regretting the break-up already?"

"No I'm not!" I said determinedly. "*This* time I'm not going to forgive him. This is the new me — the complete, new, self-contained me. He can snap his fingers until they fall off, but I'm not going to come running."

Matt was bouncing the football on the spot now, watching me out of the corner of his eye all the time. "As I said, I'll believe that when I see it. In fact, we'll have a bet on it: a pound says you'll be back with him by the end of the week!"

"You're on!" I said. "You can give me a pound if I'm not."

Matt carried on bouncing, I looked at my watch. "Look, I've got to go," I said. "I'm supposed to go round to Jen's at eleven."

Matt deftly bounced the ball from his knee straight into his sports bag. "See you," he said. "And if I see you with *him* inside seven days you owe me a pound."

"You won't!" I smiled as I turned away. I walked on down the road and when I

I CAME out of our block of flats and bumped straight into Matt. He studied me from arm's length and then raised an eyebrow knowingly.

"Don't tell me," he sighed. "It's happened again?"

I nodded and we paused outside the entrance. I was going to my friend Jen's house, and Matt, judging from the gear he was wearing, was going to football practice.

"How did you know?" I asked bleakly.

"Easy. You've got the old 'I've-had-a-row-with-Simon' look on. It's sort of grey with tinges of black around the edges."

I looked at Matt bleakly. "This time, it's the end."

He smiled and shook his head. "If I had a pound for every time I've heard you say that . . ."

"I *mean* it," I insisted.

"You always mean it," he said, and his mouth went down a little at the corners. That was strange for Matt, because he was the type who was always grinning and fooling around. You know — the big brother type. He'd asked me out once, long ago. I'd burst into incredulous giggles and he'd said quickly that he'd only been joking, of *course* he hadn't meant it.

"This time I've had enough," I said, thrusting my hands deep into my pockets out of the cold. "He took me to the town hall disco last night and spent the entire evening chatting to the girl in the cloakroom — said she was his sister's friend."

Matt's eyes twinkled. "His sister's got an awful lot of friends."

"Don't I know it?" Saying he was only talking to girls because they were 'his sister's friends' was a regular excuse of Simon's. I sighed; if only he wasn't so good-looking, if only girls didn't fall all over him, if only he was just ordinary, a bit more like Matt.

"That's a big sigh," Matt said. He took the football out of his sports bag, threw it up

TO YOU

reached the corner I looked back. He was standing quite still, watching me. I waved and he waved — then I went on to Jen's.

I had to pass Simon's house on the way into town and though I crossed to the other side of the road and even though I made a point of looking straight ahead, I was horribly aware of him being very close. I bit my lip; *somehow* I had to get over him. I'd been going out with him for seven months — and it seemed he'd been messing me about the whole time. I'd never really been sure of him.

Jen was sitting on the wall outside her house, waiting for me. I tried to smile, really I did, I tried to look happy, but she took one look at my face and groaned.

"Don't tell me," she said. "It's happened again?"

The following Saturday, the night of the disco, I was definitely weakening. I'd been OK all week and had kept myself busy. But I had discovered that having someone of my own, even if he was totally unreliable, was, for some crazy reason, preferable to having no-one. I'd heard from different sources that Simon had been seen at the cinema with 'his sister's friend' on Tuesday, then the following two days had reports that he'd been seen alone, in town, looking really miserable.

Miserable without *me* was a tempting prospect. Was he regretting what had happened? Was he unhappy without me? Could it be that this time he'd really be different?

"Now, you're not going to go off with Simon at the disco and leave me, are you?" Jen said when she came round for me in the evening.

"'Course I'm not!" I tried to look shocked. "Anyway, he might not be there."

"He's always there — hoping to spot the new talent," she said dourly. She didn't like him much!

I shrugged. "Maybe he's got other plans now. Perhaps he's seeing her," I said, but the last few words stuck painfully in my throat. It would be even worse if he was with her at the disco and I'd have to stand around all night and watch him dance with her.

"We'll see," she said.

We finished getting ready and set off. The disco was a once-weekly thing and though the town hall wasn't much cop as far as atmosphere was concerned, it was literally all there was going on, so nearly everyone in town under 21 turned up.

Matt was standing by the door when we arrived. I was really pleased to see him — anything to put off the awful moment when I had to look round and maybe see Simon with someone else.

"You owe me a pound!" I said. "Seven whole days and I'm still a single girl."

"Not quite," he said.

"What d'you mean?"

"It's seven days tomorrow. It was Sunday we had the bet."

"What's twenty-four hours?"

"A lot," he said. "Especially as Simon's here tonight *and* he's on his own."

I felt a wave of relief sweep over me — and then I remembered that I didn't care and shrugged. "So what?" I said.

Matt looked at me steadily. "I know you, Marcy," he said. "You can't fool me."

He gave me such a strange, meaningful look that my breath caught in my throat and I didn't speak. For a moment our eyes locked and then Jen tugged at my arm and broke the spell.

"Come and dance," she said. "It's like a morgue in here — we need to get them all going a bit."

I dragged my eyes away from Matt's. "See you!" I said cheerfully, but he didn't reply.

wasn't getting through to me as easily as before.

"You know there's no one else, really."

"You've got a funny way of showing it . . ."

He looked at me appealingly. "Look, I know I'm a bit of a flirt but . . . well, when it comes down to it, it's you I really care about. Come on, soften up a bit." He stroked my cheek with an expert hand, rested his head against mine. Over his shoulder I saw Jen shaking her head in resignation. We turned slowly, moving to the music.

"It's OK, isn't it; we're friends again. I know we have these little bust-ups but . . ."

Matt came into view and he was staring at me with such a strange expression on his face — a bit puzzled, a bit resigned and a bit sad. I froze and didn't hear the rest of what Simon was saying. We danced round and Matt disappeared. I knew his eyes were on me, though, I could feel them. Something weird was happening to me, something I'd never even suspected could . . .

I was finished with Simon now — and to prove I meant it there was a bet on.

I spotted Simon about five seconds after Jen and I started dancing. He was with a couple of his mates, they were standing up by the bar looking at a crowd of girls and calling out to them. He was wearing a dark shirt and white jacket, and with his blondish hair he looked — I've got to say it — pretty good. He pretended not to see me, but I knew he had.

I looked from him back to Jen, my eyes bleak.

"Will you leave off?" she hissed. "If you go back to him he's just going to make a fool of you all over again. Where's your pride, girl?"

"Don't know," I muttered, weakly.

Three dances later he started to walk across towards us.

"Don't you dare!" Jen hissed.

"Just one dance," I said. "What's the harm in that?"

"You're impossible!" she said, and she flounced off and left me to it — just as Simon got to my side, put one arm round my waist and another over my shoulder.

"I've missed you," he whispered into my ear.

"Really?" I said coolly. Well, it was meant to sound cool, I don't know how it came out. "What about your sister's friend, didn't she console you?"

"She was nothing. You know that, don't you?"

"Do I?" I was keeping up the barrier and somehow, *somehow* it was working. He

". . . so next week I thought we could go to this place that I know and . . . Hey, are you listening to me?"

I moved back from Simon's shoulder, from his smooth, insistent tone. "No," I said. "Not really."

"But you . . ."

"I've got to go!" I said suddenly. "Someone owes me some money."

His good-looking face creased into a frown so that he just looked cross and spoilt. "What're you talking about?" he asked impatiently.

"A bet!" I said. "Excuse me." I wriggled myself out of his arms and left him standing in the middle of the dance floor. It was probably the first time that he'd ever been abandoned, and he was lost!

I walked straight over to Matt. Everything was suddenly crystal clear.

"About that pound," I said, and he looked at me uncertainly.

"You're back with him, then? You've come to give it to me?"

I smiled and shook my head. "You owe me the pound. I'm not going back."

He looked at me hopefully, yet he hesitated — almost as if he was scared to ask. "Not . . . not ever?"

"Not ever," I said. "This is it — goodbye Simon!"

"Hello Matt?" he asked, tentatively.

"Hello, Matt," I echoed softly, and we smiled at each other. It was all I said — but then it was all I needed to say . . .

All of us do stupid things from time to time which leave us with egg firmly on our faces! Sometimes there's only one way out of these awkward situations and that's lying! Everyone knows about white lies, the ones that often stop other people's feelings being hurt. But what about the grey ones? The ones we use to cover up when we've goofed — and been found out! Especially if it concerns boyfriends and parents.

Well stay calm. Thanks to Patches there's no need to scramble round looking for excuses to use in these emergencies — we've got them here!

Oh Boy!

The thing about boys in general is, they're very gullible — which means they're easily fooled. Their minds, if they have any, tend to work differently from ours — as a rule, they'll actually *believe* what you tell them. Poor things!

So, when you turn up late for a date for the third time running, tell him you've got something really special to give him. The reason you're late is, you actually came out without it, but went *all* the way back to get it. Then present him with some loving little gift — even if it's just a lock of your hair (washed, of course!) or a loving little poem about him. He'll feel too rotten to sulk or moan any further. He might even end up apologising to you!

Now, when he wants to see you one night, and you just don't fancy it (or you've got something better to do) it's often best just to say

something simple like : your long-lost auntie's coming to visit and you have to stay in and see her. (He definitely won't want to join the family reunion!) Or even say you've simply *got* to wash your hair that night. Your average guy won't usually argue with something like that — they actually believe it takes us a *whole* night!

But . . . what if the persistent chap decides to phone to see how you're getting on and you're out painting the town red with your mates? Don't panic — just ask casually : didn't he know that while you're waiting for your Deep-Conditioning -Hair-Treatment-Oil to work, you always go out for a run, and that's why you couldn't come to the phone? He'll probably think, "Wow, aren't girls fascinating!" and be too flummoxed to question you any further.

You can get into even deeper waters than this, though — for example, when your guy, or his best mate sees you out with another bloke — in an uncharacteristic moment of weakness, of course! This can be dicey — he may really become suspicious.

If you actually *like* your guy and would quite like to hold on to him, you'll have to spin him some complicated tale — a simple, "He's my cousin from Australia," or, "He actually fancies my sister and wanted to ask me all about her," just won't do. But if you were to say, calmly, that your dad, being a strong supporter of the Society for the Protection of British Water Buffalo offered a night

out with you as the first prize in a fund-raising raffle, could he really object to your helping such a good cause?

If you haven't quite got the brass neck for all that, just say yes, he *was* an ex-boyfriend of yours, and when you split up, he owed you some money. And the only way he'd pay you back was if you went out with him for a last time. While your current guy's gasping for breath at the sheer improbability of the story, you can add that you only wanted the money back so *you* could treat *him* to a night out for a change. Then your next move's to think up a good excuse for borrowing some cash from your mum . . . (We didn't say it was easy!)

Parents — Honestly!

Parents are funny — they're not really like boyfriends at all — well would *you* go out with them? The main problem is they're not easily convinced — of

anything! In fact, to be honest, parents are really a rather suspicious lot, and if you do anything at all *naughty*, they'll usually find you out — often by telepathy!

But if they should happen to stop for breath while yelling at you, locking you in your room, or bundling you out the back door for ever, you might as well try to fob them off with *some* excuse . . . or die fighting, as we say in the Patches office.

Imagine, for instance, that in a mad moment of fun, you and your mate decide to go off and have the colour of your hair changed to a nice pink, or lilac. An innocent enough idea — to you. Yet some suspicious parents will see this as the first step of your decline into total badness and decadent living.

But if you quickly explain that you'd actually gone to have the short, wavy, bouncy perm that your mum's been wanting you to have for years, only it went terribly

EMERG

Yes, we've done it again! You've got yourself into trouble and we've got the excuses to help you out! What a team.

wrong — they might simmer down just long enough for you to escape. And it's better than just standing there being murdered!

You could tell them you're writing up a project on "minority groups in Britain today" and you wanted to find out what it's like to stand out from the crowd, and feel different — thus your new hair. They might even end up admiring your courage.

Another strange thing about parents is their obsession with Time. Of course, you'll usually obey their 10.30 curfew, but on the odd occasion when you find yourself coming through the door and it's gone midnight, try these . . .

. . . the music broke down at the party/disco and didn't come on till 10.30, so you only actually had one hour's dancing then you had to leave . . .

. . . on your way home at your usual time you discovered you'd left your handbag on the bus, so you had to walk all the way to the bus depot to get it back — and you're, snivel, sob, exhausted . . .

. . . you found a lost kitten with an injured leg, but, knowing what they'd say if you brought it home, you went wandering all over town till you found a 24-hour Cat Shelter . . .

A last word of caution, though — there's no point in spinning your parents *any* of these yarns unless you're the oldest one in the family. 'Cos they'll have heard them all before! So if you're the baby we're sorry, but you'll just have to be good!

ANOTHER RAINY DAY..

YOU LOOK OUT OF THE WINDOW AND YOUR HEART SINKS — IT'S POURING WITH RAIN! BUT DON'T DESPAIR, BECAUSE PATCHES IS HERE TO BRIGHTEN UP YOUR LIFE! TRY ANY ONE OF THESE IDEAS TO CHASE THE BLUES AWAY . . .

● Write down the names of everyone you know — you'll be surprised at the length of the list.

● Crawl everywhere! Everyone'll think you've gone mad!

● Count the raindrops on your window. Then make bets with your friends on the raindrops running down the pane. First to the windowsill's the winner.

● Read through all your old diaries and Valentine cards.

● Go for a walk in the rain with your boyfriend and huddle very close together under one small umbrella.

● Raid the attic — but take supplies of food and Coke. You never know when you'll emerge again . . .

● Have the longest bath in history. Take everything you need into the bathroom with you — bath oil, soap, shampoo and talc. Include sandwiches, biscuits, a flask of tea — then lie back and have a tremendous soak!

● Paint your toenails electric blue or flashing apricot!

● Concoct your own "rain cake" and bake it every rainy day.

● Go for a sauna.

● Make an "Oxfam Pile." Go through all your clothes and put the ones you never wear to one side. Someone'll be grateful for them.

● Sort through your make-up bag, throwing out all the yukky, horrible shades and clean your bag. Keep the lipsticks, though.

● Now you can melt down all those old lipsticks and make a new shade.

● Phone up all your friends and tell them to put on bright macs and wellies, then go out singing in the rain!

● Clean the inside of your bedroom window and watch the outside being cleaned for you by the rain.

● Write to all the people you haven't written to for ages.

● Find a quiet corner and meditate.

● Get out all the soppy records you own and have a good weep. See if you can beat the raindrops with your tears . . .

● Wear bright yellow clothes and sunglasses and pretend you're in a tropical heatwave.

● Dress up in your bright red/yellow mac and wellies and go for a paddle in the puddles.

● Get out your mum's box of old photos and have a good laugh. Then sort out your own photos and fill your album up.

● Call your friends and invite them over to your place. Then spend the day making each other up and changing your hairstyles.

● Get out that box of paints that's been lying at the back of the cupboard and try your hand at painting.

Either get some henna or a toner or rinse and put it on your hair. Leave it on as long as possible and you'll never go unnoticed again!

● Tidy your bedroom and rearrange it at the same time. This might sound totally boring but it will pass the time and you'll be amazed at how good your room looks.

● This is a follow-on from number six. Look under your bed and you'll find everything that's been lost since last year. Count all the items.

● Put on your youngest-looking clothes and go to a children's matinee. Join in the jokes and laughter and eat plenty of ice-cream.

● Raid your mum's sewing basket and make a cushion out of scraps of fabric. Then you can get rid of all your old, holey tights when you stuff it!

● Search high and low and get all your old copies of Patches together. Then cover them with a colourful binder using bright cardboard, glue and a bit of imagination.

● Bake some "character" biscuits — gingerbread men, snowmen, animals — as many different shapes as possible.

● Go through all your records, separating the albums and singles; clean them well and catalogue them.

● Go through all your clothes to check if they're in good condition or whether they could do with a wash. If there are any buttons loose, hems coming down, etc. — mend them!

● Get your old T-shirts together and dye them bright colours.

● Curl up on the settee and have a nice doze. Pretend you're the cat!

● Play some good, fast records and exercise to them. Bend as much as possible — really makes those lazy muscles work.

● Practise with your make-up in front of the mirror. Try to be professional — blend all those colours in well, and remember to use brushes!

● If you've got long hair, put it into as many tiny plaits as you can and leave them in for as long as possible. When you take them out, your hair'll be lovely and wavy.

● Get a simple bread recipe and make it. Once you've done the dough you could use it for rolls. Make as many unusual shapes as possible — plaiting, knotting the dough, etc. They look great when they're baked!

● Go through all your old Patches and cut out all your favourite pictures. Paste them to a large sheet of card or stiff paper and hang it on your wall. The collage effect'll be terrific!

● Write some poetry. But don't just stick to soppy love poems — try as many different kinds as possible.

● Get out all your favourite postcards and birthday cards and cover the top of an old chest-of-drawers or table with them, then put clear Contact on top. Then stand back and admire it.

● Experiment with your make-up. Give yourself a rainbow face, 'cos you often see a rainbow when it rains!

● Write down all the little things you need to do like watering the plants, cleaning your make-up brushes, hemming your trousers, then tear it up and relax!

● Read a book.

● Give yourself a face-pack using the white of an egg and then try to smile. Watch the cracks!

● Draw a self-portrait but be honest! Try to get it as true to life as possible.

● Make a chart and write everyone's birthdays on it so you don't forget them.

● Make up your bed so tightly that you have to squeeze into it at night.

● Clean every single pair of shoes you own.

● Find the biggest jigsaw puzzle in the house and do it.

EVERLASTING LOVE

Colin had found the old pendant in an antique shop, and he thought it would make a perfect present for Ann . . .

HAPPY BIRTHDAY!

OH, COLIN, THANK YOU. IT'S BEAUTIFUL!

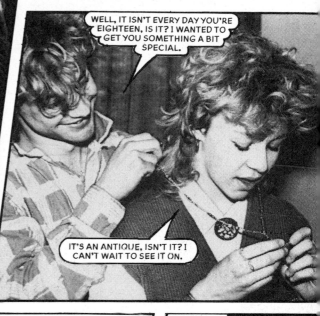

WELL, IT ISN'T EVERY DAY YOU'RE EIGHTEEN, IS IT? I WANTED TO GET YOU SOMETHING A BIT SPECIAL.

IT'S AN ANTIQUE, ISN'T IT? I CAN'T WAIT TO SEE IT ON.

But when Ann put the pendant round her neck . . .

AS LONG AS I WEAR IT, I'LL FEEL THAT YOU'RE WITH ME, NO MATTER HOW FAR APART WE MIGHT BE . . .

WH-WHAT'S HAPPENING? I FEEL DIZZY.

A picture of a field had suddenly flashed through her mind . . .

And at the same time . . .

I HAD SUCH A TERRIBLE FEELING OF SADNESS JUST NOW. BUT WHY? I SHOULD BE REALLY HAPPY.

ARE YOU OK, LOVE? FOR A MINUTE, YOU LOOKED LIKE YOU WERE GOING TO CRY.

I—I'M FINE, COLIN. I SUPPOSE I JUST GET A BIT EMOTIONAL ABOUT BIRTHDAYS.

THE SADNESS HAS GONE NOW. IT WENT AWAY AS SOON AS I TOOK OFF THE PENDANT.

COME ON — LET'S GET THIS BIRTHDAY CELEBRATION STARTED. I'VE BOOKED A TABLE AT THE POSHEST RESTAURANT IN TOWN. ARE YOU GOING TO WEAR YOUR NEW PENDANT TONIGHT?

NO, I'M NOT DRESSED UP ENOUGH FOR IT. BUT I REALLY LOVE IT, COLIN — HONESTLY.

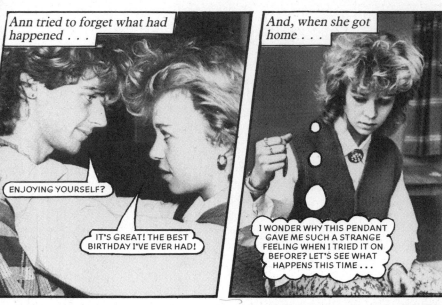

Ann tried to forget what had happened . . .

ENJOYING YOURSELF?

IT'S GREAT! THE BEST BIRTHDAY I'VE EVER HAD!

And, when she got home . . .

I WONDER WHY THIS PENDANT GAVE ME SUCH A STRANGE FEELING WHEN I TRIED IT ON BEFORE? LET'S SEE WHAT HAPPENS THIS TIME . . .

It was the same as before. There was the mental picture of the field — and the same feeling of sadness . . .

BUT AS SOON AS I TAKE IT OFF, THE SADNESS GOES AWAY. I JUST DON'T UNDERSTAND IT.

WHY SHOULD I KEEP PICTURING THAT FIELD? AND WHY DO I FEEL SO SAD? I KNOW IT'S SOMEHOW CONNECTED WITH THE PENDANT . . .

She decided to tell Colin about it . . .

IT'S REALLY STRANGE. I'VE HAD THE PENDANT FOR A WEEK NOW, AND THE SAME THING'S HAPPENED EVERY TIME I PUT IT ON. I — I JUST WISH I KNEW WHERE THAT FIELD IS . . .

IT MIGHT NOT EVEN BE A REAL PLACE, ANN. AND SUPPOSE YOU DID MANAGE TO FIND IT — WHAT GOOD WOULD IT DO?

YOU DON'T UNDERSTAND. IT — IT'S JUST THAT THE FEELING OF SADNESS I GET IS SO STRONG . . . I'VE GOT TO KNOW THE REASON FOR IT.

But . . .

WHICH ANTIQUE SHOP DID YOU BUY THE PENDANT IN? MAYBE THEY COULD TELL US SOMETHING ABOUT IT.

ALL RIGHT, WE'LL GO AND ASK. BUT IF THEY DON'T KNOW ANYTHING, WE JUST LET THE SUBJECT DROP. OK?

THAT WASN'T MUCH HELP. THE MAN SAID HE PICKED IT UP AT AN AUCTION A FEW MONTHS AGO, BUT HE'S NO IDEA WHO OWNED IT BEFORE THEN.

WELL, WE TRIED. SERIOUSLY THOUGH, ANN, I DON'T LIKE THE WAY THIS THING'S STARTING TO WORRY YOU SO MUCH. DO US BOTH A FAVOUR AND FORGET ABOUT IT, WILL YOU?

IT'S ONLY AN OLD PENDANT. WE'VE MORE IMPORTANT THINGS THAN THAT TO THINK ABOUT, HAVEN'T WE?

I SUPPOSE SO . . .

But she couldn't stop thinking about it . . .

I WONDER IF OBJECTS CAN STORE UP MEMORIES AND EMOTIONS FROM THE PAST, JUST THE WAY PEOPLE DO? MAYBE SOMETHING TERRIBLE HAPPENED IN THAT FIELD AND THIS PENDANT WAS CONNECTED WITH IT.

Days passed and every time Ann put the pendant round her neck she saw that same vision of the field . . .

Until one night . . .

IT WAS DIFFERENT THIS TIME. THERE WAS A GIRL CRYING IN THE FIELD. AND THE FEELING OF SADNESS WAS STRONGER THAN EVER. WHAT ON EARTH IS HAPPENING!

And when Colin came round to see her . . .

I'VE NEVER FELT ANYTHING LIKE IT, COLIN. I DIDN'T KNOW ANYONE COULD BE SO SAD . . .

LOOK, THIS THING'S GONE TOO FAR. IT'S GETTING TO BE AN OBSESSION WITH YOU! YOU'RE LETTING IT TAKE OVER YOUR WHOLE LIFE.

YOU'RE NEVER TOO YOUNG!

Your number's up! Whatever your age we know what you can get up to — and it's all legal!

ZERO — Even when you were still in your nappies you could have a bank account, a building society account — and you could own Premium Bonds. Wow!

FIVE — You could knock back the odd glass of sherry in private! If you could open the bottle! And you could insist (if nobody else was insisting!) on having full-time education.

TEN — Providing it could be proved you understood the difference between right and wrong, you could be convicted of a criminal offence. Of course if you were smart enough to keep insisting you didn't know what you'd done was wrong (and got yourself believed) everybody would have a pretty hard time trying to make up their minds what to do with you!

TWELVE — You can buy a pet puma (or pussy-cat!) without one of your parents or a guardian being with you.

Reached *THIRTEEN?* Then you can get what's called a 'light' part-time job for up to two hours a day on a school day or Sunday. On Saturdays, though, you can work up to eight hours. The money's rolling in!

FOURTEEN onwards you not only have rights — you have responsibilities! (Headaches start here!)

At 14, you can be convicted of a crime (and playing as dumb as you did at 10 won't work!). You can have your fingerprints taken if a magistrate says you must, or if you agree.

You can even own an air rifle or a shotgun. You can pawn goods. You can get in to an AA film. You can go into a pub — but you CAN'T buy or drink alcohol there. But you have to pay full fare on public transport, unless you use a school bus to a school more than three miles from your home.

From *FIFTEEN* you can be sent to borstal — presumably for using the shotgun you had when you were 14!

SIXTEEN (a ripe old age). You can:

leave school;

get a full-time job;

get married (provided one of your parents, a guardian or a court agrees);

you can join a union;

you can claim social security and supplementary benefit in case 1. happens but 2. doesn't! (This may change so check your local DHSS for updated info.);

you can drink alcohol in a pub or restaurant, *BUT ONLY* if you're having a meal there;

you can ruin your health (and your income) and smoke cigarettes;

you can choose your own doctor and agree to your own medical treatment without your parents or guardian being involved.

you've to pay the full prescription charges, though, unless you're still at school or on social security;

you can choose your own religion;

you can get a driving licence for a moped or motorbike;

AND you can have a passport — but only if your parents or guardian sign the application form! (Seems a bit cock-eyed when you think of all the other things you can do without 'em.)

You can also:

buy fireworks;

buy Premium Bonds;

and become a scrap-metal dealer.

SEVENTEEN, and life gets even more complicated. You can go into a betting shop — but what's the point when you can't place a bet?

You can become a street trader;

with the consent of your parents or guardian, you can join the Armed Forces;

you can hold a driving licence for any kind of vehicle except a heavy goods vehicle,

and you can go to prison if you're convicted of a serious crime — such as crooked street-trading!

EIGHTEEN, and it all happens. You can leave home without anybody's consent, and get married if you want to.

You can vote;

sit on a jury;

get a cheque card,

a credit card,

and see an X film.

You can also:

make your will;

act as an executor for somebody else's will;

be a blood donor;

change your name;

apply for a passport;

have hire purchase;

have a mortgage;

own land, property and shares;

sign contracts;

sue and be sued;

drink alcohol in pubs and anywhere else you feel like it;

work in a bar;

make bets;

apply to see your birth certificate if you're adopted;

and — tough luck — you have to pay for dental treatment!

TWENTY-ONE — Congratulations on reaching this far and getting the key to the door! PLUS you can:

stand for Parliament,

and the local council;

become a landlady,

hold a licence to sell alcohol and hold a heavy goods vehicle licence, probably to drive the beer lorry!

And that's it until you get your pension but we'll save that for another time. After all, it's still a day or two away yet!

42

I WISH I'D NEVER GIVEN YOU THE STUPID THING. LOOK, WHY DON'T YOU LET ME GET RID OF IT?

NO! YOU CAN'T DO THAT!

BUT IT'S ONLY MAKING YOU UNHAPPY. IT'S ALL YOU EVER THINK ABOUT!

I'M SORRY, COLIN. I DON'T SUPPOSE I'M MUCH FUN TO BE WITH THESE DAYS, AM I?

WE USED TO BE HAPPY BEFORE YOU STARTED THINKING AND TALKING ABOUT THAT PENDANT ALL THE TIME. SO HERE'S WHAT WE'RE GOING TO DO — ON SATURDAY WE'LL TAKE A BUS MILES OUT INTO THE COUNTRY, RIGHT AWAY FROM EVERYTHING. WE'LL HAVE A PICNIC, JUST THE TWO OF US. AND NO TALK ABOUT PENDANTS . . . NO TALK ABOUT ANYTHING EXCEPT OURSELVES! IS IT A DEAL?

So, on Saturday . . .

WE'RE GOING TO HAVE A GREAT TIME TODAY.

YES, I'VE BEEN LOOKING FORWARD TO IT.

But as the bus was travelling along a country road . . .

COLIN — LOOK! THERE'S THE FIELD I'VE BEEN GETTING THOSE PICTURES OF! I RECOGNISE THAT TREE!

I'VE GOT TO GET OFF HERE! I HAVE TO GO TO THAT FIELD!

DON'T BE STUPID, ANN. WHAT ABOUT OUR PICNIC?

I DON'T CARE ABOUT THE PICNIC! I'VE GOT TO GO TO THAT FIELD. I KNOW THAT'S WHERE THE ANSWER IS . . .

THIS WAS SUPPOSED TO BE A SPECIAL DAY FOR US! WHAT'S MORE IMPORTANT TO YOU — ME, OR THAT PENDANT?

IF YOU GET OFF HERE, YOU GET OFF ON YOUR OWN. I CAN'T TAKE ANY MORE OF THIS STUPID OBSESSION OF YOURS!

THEN I'M SORRY, COLIN. BUT THIS IS SOMETHING I HAVE TO DO.

HE'S GONE. OH, COLIN. I HOPED YOU'D UNDERSTAND.

I DON'T EVEN KNOW WHAT I'M LOOKING FOR, BUT THERE MUST BE AN EXPLANATION SOMEWHERE.

Then . . .

OH — YOU STARTLED ME, DEAR. IT ISN'T OFTEN I BUMP INTO ANYONE ELSE WHEN I'M OUT FOR MY WALK.

I'M SORRY. I DIDN'T REALISE THERE WAS ANYONE ELSE HERE, EITHER.

IT'S A LOVELY SPOT, ISN'T IT? DO YOU LIVE NEAR HERE?

YES. I COME FOR A WALK IN THE FIELD EVERY DAY. SOMETIMES I'LL JUST SIT IN THIS SPOT FOR HOURS. I — I'VE NOTHING MUCH ELSE TO DO NOWADAYS, YOU SEE.

MY HOUSE IS JUST DOWN THE LANE. WOULD YOU LIKE TO COME BACK FOR A CUP OF TEA? I LIVE ON MY OWN AND I DON'T GET MANY VISITORS.

WELL, IF YOU'RE SURE I WON'T BE INTRUDING . . .

SHE SEEMS A BIT LONELY. I DON'T LIKE TO REFUSE.

The old lady said her name was Miss Vernon . . .

YOU DON'T COME FROM AROUND HERE, DO YOU, MY DEAR? WHAT BROUGHT YOU DOWN HERE TODAY?

I'M NOT SURE MYSELF. I JUST HAD A SILLY IDEA THAT I MIGHT FIND THE ANSWER TO A MYSTERY HERE.

But, at the old lady's house . . .

OH! THAT PHOTOGRAPH!

AND YOU CAN TAKE BACK YOUR STUPID PENDANT, ALEC TRENT!

"We both walked away in anger, leaving the pendant where it had fallen in the field . . ."

BUT THE DAY BEFORE ALEC WAS DUE TO SAIL FOR FRANCE, WE HAD A STUPID QUARREL. WE WERE IN THE FIELD AT THE TIME, AND I WAS SO ANGRY I TOOK THE PENDANT OFF AND THREW IT AT HIM . . .

NO, THANKS. I DON'T WANT ANYTHING THAT MIGHT REMIND ME OF YOU!

"When I woke up the next day, I regretted the argument. But when I went back to the field to fetch the pendant, I couldn't find it . . ."

IT'S GONE. SOMEONE ELSE MUST HAVE PICKED IT UP . . .

I TOLD ALEC HE'D ALWAYS BE WITH ME WHILE I WORE THE PENDANT. NOW THAT I'VE LOST IT, I — I'VE GOT THE STRANGEST FEELING. IT'S AS IF WE'RE BEING PARTED FOREVER.

So . . .

I'VE GOT TO WRITE TO ALEC. I'VE GOT TO TELL HIM I STILL LOVE HIM . . .

"But he never got my letter . . ."

IT'S FROM THE WAR OFFICE. ALEC'S BEEN KILLED IN ACTION . . . OH NO . . . NO . . . !

"Of course, I blamed myself . . ."

IT WAS BECAUSE I DIDN'T HAVE THE PENDANT. WHEN I LOST IT, I — I LOST ALEC TOO . . .

THERE COULD NEVER BE ANOTHER LOVE IN MY LIFE AFTER ALEC. I'VE SPENT YEARS REGRETTING THE MISTAKE I MADE. I EVEN BOUGHT THIS HOUSE, SO THAT I COULD BE NEAR THE FIELD . . .

OH, MISS VERNON, I'M SO SORRY. NOW I UNDERSTAND WHY I KEPT PICTURING THE FIELD AND WHY I GOT SUCH A STRONG FEELING OF SADNESS FROM THE PENDANT . . .

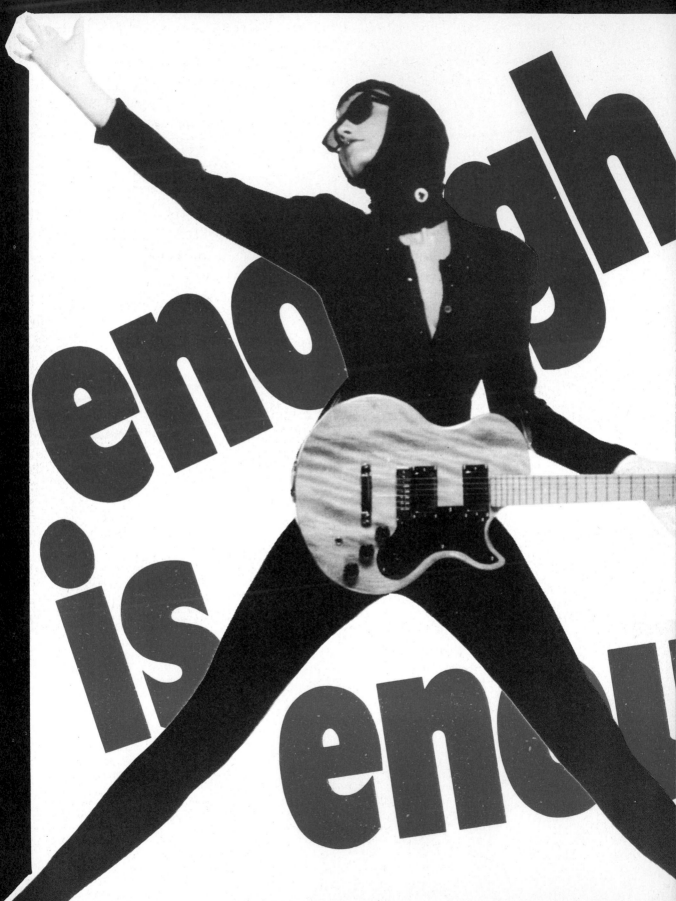

enough

eno is enou

. . . so it's time to shake off those blues and start smiling again . . .

Fed up? Depressed? Just feeling down? Well, that's not helping much, is it? But the one thing that just NEVER does you any good is simply sitting around gloomily counting your toes. What's the use in that? You'll only come up with the same number every time! So how *can* you beat the blues when they do their nasty little trick of creeping up on you? Well, we've got a few ideas you might like to try — just read on!

SCREAM

No, no, I don't mean here and now! After all, a crowded bus or the back of Miss Watson's maths class isn't exactly private, is it? And you don't want everyone to know you're fed up, do you? Choose somewhere you can really let go and scream as loudly as you can—preferably disturbing as few people as possible. What about when your little brother has all his pals round, or when your mum's engrossed in Dallas? They'll never notice the extra noise — believe me ... Mind you, on second thoughts, perhaps a silent scream is better. All you have to do there is open your mouth and make sure no sound comes out. Difficult, isn't it? But you'll feel better 'cos you'll have tensed your muscles, got the adrenalin flowing, and then relaxed everything again. It'll be such a relief to stop that you'll feel 100% better immediately!

LOCK YOURSELF IN THE BATHROOM

Try this one if screaming fails. It's a bit drastic, but it does work! Wash your face and the back of your neck repeatedly in very cold water until you're physically shivering. Keep on with this, but at the same time run a very *warm* bath, pour in some scented bath oil (or some baby oil and a few drops of perfume if you're broke). Now, take off all your clothes (this bit is VERY important so don't forget) and when you're so cold that you can't stand it anymore — leap into the sweet-smelling warm water. If you've forgotten to take your clothes off you'll only be more depressed, but if you've followed our instructions you'll be so glad to heat up again that you'll forget all about feeling blue in the first place!

CUT YOUR HAIR

The problem with this one is that it could make you happy, but it could also

make you feel like jumping under a bus! If you don't want to cut it yourself and can't afford a quick trip to the local hairdressers, why not get somebody else to cut it for you? They may make a brilliant job of it and really surprise you, or they could make such a complete disaster of it that you'll be so angry you'll forget to be depressed! What d'you mean, it's a crazy idea? I thought it made perfect sense!

WRITE LETTERS OF COMPLAINT

This is a good one, but make sure you have loads of paper and three pens handy 'cos you could get carried away. Write to everybody under the sun you've ever wanted to say something to, but never had the nerve — your mum, dad, budgie, teacher, bus conductor, boyfriend ... Tell them precisely what you think of them and *why*. Now you'll realise why you needed three pens! Then re-read carefully what you've written — and start making confetti out of the paper! You'll have cramp in your fingers and feel like a twit, but you won't be blue any more 'cos you'll have gotten it all out of your system!

DO A GOOD DEED FOR THE DAY

Tell your mum you're leaving home. By the time she's finished yelling and telling you what an incompetent idiot you are, and how you couldn't boil an egg by yourself, you'll be so depressed that you'll have forgotten what originally made you feel the way you were feeling! You'll also be so relieved to be tucked up, cosy and well fed at home that you'll end up feeling good!

RING UP AN OLD BOYFRIEND

Try to pick one who was particularly rotten to you, though. This works best, 'cos once you start chatting about old times you'll start to remember the nights he stood you up, the two timing and the tears ... It will come as such a relief that you're no longer going out with him that your depression will lift instantly! If you can't face ringing him, try digging out your old diary—that should put you straight, too. Now get out there and meet someone nice — you deserve to!

CHANGE YOUR HABITS

Don't just get talked into going to the same old disco with the same old

crowd every Saturday night. That won't help. You need to grab your courage in both hands and do something different. Take yourself to that picture you've always wanted to see but no-one else ever fancied. Splash out your savings on a pizza instead of chips — and roll home in style in a taxi instead of running for the last bus! At least you'll have done something for *yourself* (and by yourself) for a change. You might even find that you like it!

WRITE A POEM

Go absolutely wild with all the romantic images you can think of. Then read it to yourself as if somebody else had written it especially for you. You'll either burst into tears because nobody loves you that much, or laugh yourself silly at how corny it sounds — either way, you're guaranteed a change of mood!

CHANGE YOUR DIET

Crisps, chocolates and sugary drinks will not only help your spots thrive, but add inches to your thighs and tummy, turn your hair lank and greasy, and probably give you an allergic reaction which will result in headaches and severe depression. If you are sane, sensible, slim and spotless — move over to this kind of diet immediately. You'll definitely have something to be blue about in a very short time!

TAKE UP A HOBBY

No, I'm not talking about badminton or knitting. Go for something a lot more sensational, like hang-gliding, belly-dancing or North African cookery. At least it'll give you something interesting to talk about. (And you never know who you might jump off a mountain and glide into!)

But whatever else you do, or don't do, try being positive for a change. Everybody gets blue now and again, and it doesn't actually do any harm to sit down and let the feeling wash over you. After all, indulging yourself for half-an-hour can't do any harm. But when you find that the half-hour turns into days, or weeks, it's time to pick yourself up, give yourself a shake — and get on with your life. Use a few of our tips if you like, or make up some of your own — it shouldn't be long before you're smiling again!

BUT AT LEAST I CAN GIVE IT BACK TO YOU NOW.

THANK YOU, MY DEAR. THAT MEANS A GREAT DEAL TO ME.

IT'S STRANGE . . . BUT SUDDENLY I FEEL AS IF ALEC IS WITH ME AGAIN, AFTER ALL THESE YEARS.

When Ann left the house . . .

POOR MISS VERNON. WHAT A TERRIBLE LIFE SHE'S HAD — ALL BECAUSE OF ONE STUPID QUARREL . . .

Then . . .

WHERE'VE YOU BEEN, ANN? I'VE BEEN LOOKING EVERYWHERE FOR YOU!

COLIN! WHAT ARE YOU DOING HERE? I THOUGHT YOU'D STAYED ON THE BUS.

I GOT OFF AT THE NEXT STOP AND CAME BACK TO LOOK FOR YOU. I LOVE YOU, ANN. IT WOULD BE CRAZY TO LET A STUPID PENDANT SPOIL THINGS FOR US!

OH, COLIN . . .

She told him about Miss Vernon . . .

WE'VE BEEN LUCKY, HAVEN'T WE? OUR QUARREL DIDN'T END IN SADNESS, LIKE THE ONE ALEC AND CHRISTINE HAD.

TO THINK SHE'S BEEN LIVING WITH THAT MEMORY ALL THOSE YEARS! STILL, MAYBE NOW THAT SHE'S GOT THE PENDANT BACK, SHE'LL BE A LITTLE HAPPIER.

LET'S STAY IN TOUCH WITH HER, COLIN. WE COULD VISIT HER SOMETIMES — SHARE A LITTLE OF OUR OWN HAPPINESS WITH HER.

WHY NOT? WE'VE GOT ENOUGH HAPPINESS TO SPARE A LITTLE FOR A LONELY OLD LADY, HAVEN'T WE?

"But somehow, I think that today that lonely old lady feels like a young girl in love again . . ."

THE EN

RADIO NASTIES!

PATCHES TAKES A LOOK AT THE DUFF RECORDS AND BANDS OF YESTER-YEAR...

HERE'S a good game to play when you're feeling a bit bored at Christmas, in the space between opening your presents, digesting your turkey, and waiting for 'Top Of The Pops' to get under way. Of course you don't have to play it at Christmas, and the contestants don't HAVE to be Auntie Ethel and Uncle Hughie, whose idea of modern music is Pearl Carr and Teddy Johnson (ask yer mum!).

So, get yourself and a few mates in a room with a few of your big brother or sister's old singles, and you're all set!

It's simple — all you have to do is ask your mates to name the worst records they can think of, and some of the silliest band names, and of course, the real tester, the stupidest singles by the daftest groups.

Of course you'll win hands down, because you'll have studied our special Patches selection, the result of hours of sweat and hysteria in the office. Only problem is if your friends have read it as well! You'll have to hope your memory is better than theirs.

You don't want to come over too cocky to kick off with, so why not begin with a few modern cringers that everyone'll be able to remember? Anything by Black Lace is certain to get things rolling, or you could mention that you can't understand how a band came to be called A Flock Of Seagulls. Frankie Lymon and The Teenagers should raise a few eyebrows too.

Now that you've got them on the run, you can go for the big ones, like 'When I Need You' by Leo Sayer, and suggest that anyone called Leo deserves to be about four foot three, with a garden gnome voice to match!

One for the more mature relatives, sure to bring a sentimental smile to your mum's face as she pokes her nose round the door asking if anyone fancies a coffee, is The Batchelors, 'I Believe'.

AAAAAARRRRRRRRGGGGGGHHH-HHHHH!!!!!!

Football songs are always a goody, but watch that you're not having a fit over Spurs' attempts to sing, while your boyfriend quietly fumes. You'd forgotten that he thinks that Glen Hoddle is the greatest thing since sliced bread.

After a quick recovery, you can then remind everyone that The English World Cup Squad rocketed to No. 2 in 1982 with 'This Time', before crashing out of the competition, leaving us all to then remember that we were BRITISH, and pin our hopes on Scotland!

Or you could always slip in a few reminders of embarrassing pop toons made by TV personalities who're trying to forget their murky pasts, like 'Deck of Cards' by Max 'Big Money' Bygraves or 'The Floral Dance' by Terry Wogan. Both hammer anything that James Last ever did!

Fans of Jonathan King (were there any?), will of course remember 'Everyone's Gone To The Moon'. Wish HE would, eh?

Any Ultravox fans out there? Surely you're trying to forget Midge Ure's version of The Walker Brothers' hit 'No Regrets'? THEIR version is so bad it's brilliant, but poor old Midge's effort is ... well ... stinking, OK? Of course, following up a blow like that with a mention of Midge's original

band Slik, will have any 'Vienna' fans reaching for the nearest blunt object.

Names of bands are always a good giggle, and the older the better. Try mentioning a band called Elias And His Zig Zag Jive Flutes, that no-one alive will ever remember, except your granny and even she's fallen asleep while watching 'The Sound Of Music', so she won't be sticking her nose into the conversation. What about Makadopolous And His Greek Serenaders, who wowed a few hep cats back in 1960 with a song called 'Never On Sunday'.

Shane Fenton And The Fentones didn't win any prizes for originality either, and it seems that a certain Alvin Stardust was once part of this supergroup, but don't mention that to Liza Goddard!

The list goes on ... Try Frank D'Rone next time someone asks your dad's name, especially if it's your boyfriend's mum who's asking! While she's still in a state of shock, you could mention that you've always been a fan of Jimmy Glimmer And The Fireballs, and Conway Twitty's 'Is A Bluebird Blue?'. Really gets your body movin' at the Youth Club Disco!

As a finale, you should ask if there are any dreadful records AND stupid names that they know of ...

Tricky? Not if you follow the Patches' guide. Remind everyone of those golden days of the sixties, when The FleeRekkers' had everyone dancin' in the aisles with 'Green Jeans' (OK, you CAN be sick, but don't take too long over it!), or what about Javells-Featuring Nosmo King with 'Nothing To Say'?

By this time, your mates should just about be getting worried or sick or just worried sick(!) about your endless drivellings concerning groups of yester-year, so do the decent thing and put the kettle on and get the Christmas cake out, but not before you've slapped on an Echo And The Bunnymen album at full blast. Now there's a silly name! In fact, that gives me a good idea for a party game ...

MAKE

One of the biggest problems in the music business is the fact that for years men have been the ones who've been doing the rocking and rolling while the girls are only left with the pleasure of being allowed to scream at them . . .

Of course, there are exceptions to this rule and nowadays it seems that there are more and more women making appearances in the charts.

So if you don't really fancy becoming a hairdresser or a sales assistant, and feel that you'd like to do something a bit more glamorous, but don't have a clue how to go about it, then read on . . .

ARE YOU REALLY SUITED TO THE MUSIC BUSINESS?

1) Which TV programme would you most like to watch?
a) Top Of The Pops.
b) Brookside.
c) The Other Side Of The Tracks.
d) Game For A Laugh.

2) How much do you worry about your appearance?
a) A lot.
b) Quite a lot.
c) Not very much.
d) I'm sorry but I don't understand this question.

3) How would you describe yourself?
a) Out-going, intelligent and shrewd.
b) Quite normal, but don't like to say too much unnecessarily.
c) Shy, easily hurt and insecure.
d) Me? Oh, I dunno.

4) What are your favourite hobbies?
a) Going out and having a laugh with the girls.
b) Going swimming or playing tennis with your friends.
c) Reading and listening to music.
d) Lying in your bed.

5) If you were offered three albums, which set would you choose?
a) Frankie Goes To Hollywood, Duran Duran, Dead Or Alive.
b) Culture Club, Wham!, David Bowie.
c) Sade, Roxy Music, David Bowie.
d) My record player ain't got a plug on it!

6) Which of the following do you hate?
a) Being idle.
b) Not getting your own way.
c) Being forced to do things quickly.
d) Being busy.

7) When don't you bother wearing make-up?
a) When I'm sleeping.
b) When I'm going swimming etc.
c) I never wear make-up, except for when I'm going out.
d) I hate make-up.

CONCLUSIONS

MOSTLY A'S: You are pop star material! These days if someone is in the limelight because they have quite an outrageous image, then it's important for them to actually *live out* that image.

In interviews, you would probably find it quite easy to lie about a lot of things and have people believe you. The only piece of advice for you is simply to "Go For It" 'cos you're head and shoulders above the rest of the rabble . . .

MOSTLY B'S: You are quite a normal person. This isn't a problem if you want to become part of the music industry, there are lots of people who don't have to pretend! You could probably get away with quite a glamorous girl-next-door image and be adored by teenage boys and their mums!

IT BIG!

WHICH DIRECTION SHOULD I GO IN?

This may be something you've already thought about, but if not, here are a few pointers . . .

If you know exactly where your talents lie, then you have no problems, but if not, the best thing is to decide which instrument you find most attractive, and whether or not you can sing! (REMEMBER: Whatever comes out of your throat is *you!* As long as it's in tune, then there's no reason to believe that you can't sing!)

If you fancy buying a drum kit, a guitar or bass or synthesiser, then it probably makes more sense to go for the cheapest you can. That way, if you reckon it's not suited to you, you can sell it without having lost a vast amount of money.

It isn't *too* important to become an expert before you can play with anyone else. Bands can make up songs with only two chords!

WHAT DO I DO NEXT?

We're not just talking about how to form an all-girl band. It's possible for girls to take up roles in bands that are normally thought of as being specifically for males — e.g. drums or bass. Captain Sensible's backing band are all girls, as were the *Fun Boy Three's* band.

But if you do fancy the idea of being in an all-girl band, then you may be in for quite a struggle . . .

It probably won't be very easy

finding female drummers or bass players (unless these are one of the positions you fancy yourself), so you should advertise in the local press stating that you're only looking for girls. If you live in a city, then your best bet is to place ads in the classified sections of the music press. It'll be practically impossible for you to get any reaction locally if you live in a small town or village, however.

8) Which do you find most difficult?
a) Keeping your mouth shut.
b) Lying through your teeth.
c) Meeting new people.
d) Getting out of your bed.

CONCLUSIONS

MOSTLY C'S: You would really suit a career in the music business (but only if you've got talent). You're quite shy really so you would much prefer to make your music and have people appreciate that rather than the way you look or act.

It'll probably be much harder for you to get noticed in the first place, mainly because you're not too fond of meeting the people who could do you the most good, and then, when you've been given enough money, you can lock yourself in a recording studio for years on end perfecting your latest album!

MOSTLY D'S: Your head's full of mince, really! You probably have enough problems managing to think, never mind becoming a pop star!

Why not consider a career in politics?

Continued on page 56

PARTY, PARTY!

I FEEL GREAT TONIGHT! I'M REALLY GOING TO ENJOY THIS PARTY. I HOPE ALAN CLARK'S THERE.

We all know how exciting it is getting ready for a party . . .

Well, exciting for some people . . .

I WISH I COULD AFFORD TO CHANGE MY HAIRSTYLE — I LOOK ABOUT TEN WITH IT LIKE THIS. I COULD HAVE DONE WITH SOME NEW CLOTHES FOR THIS PARTY, TOO. I FEEL LIKE A REAL FRUMP!

And it's the same for boys too . . .

I HOPE THERE'S SOME DECENT GIRLS AT THIS PARTY TONIGHT. I'LL FIND THE BEST ONE ANYWAY — I LOOK GREAT!

For some boys at any rate . . .

WISH I COULD'VE AFFORDED A NEW JACKET FOR THIS PARTY — NO GIRL'S GOING TO TAKE ANY NOTICE OF ME IN THIS TATTY OLD THING! AND JUST LOOK AT THAT HAIR — WHAT A MESS!

Later . . .

HI, SUSY! YOU'RE EARLY — IT'S ONLY EIGHT O'CLOCK.

I KNOW, TRACY. I WAS JUST WONDERING IF YOU NEEDED ANY HELP IN THE KITCHEN.

I'LL PROBABLY SPEND MOST OF MY TIME IN THERE TONIGHT, ANYWAY!

AND DON'T THINK YOU'RE GOING TO HIDE IN HERE ALL NIGHT, EITHER! IT MIGHT BE MY BIRTHDAY, BUT I WANT MY PALS TO HAVE A GOOD TIME TOO! TELL YOU WHAT, I'LL INTRODUCE YOU TO MY COUSIN, LEE! HE'S REALLY GOOD-LOOKING.

OH — ER — YOU DON'T HAVE TO BOTHER.

OH, SUSY! I'M NOT ASKING YOU TO MARRY HIM! TRY TO ENJOY YOURSELF FOR ONCE!

THERE'S THE DOORBELL!

OK, OK, I'M GOING! BUT, REMEMBER, I'M GOING TO MAKE SURE YOU HAVE SOME FUN!

52

OH, I WISH I WASN'T SO SHY — PARTIES CAN BE A REAL NIGHTMARE!

Just then . . .

HEY, SUSY, THIS IS MY COUSIN, LEE.

HELLO.

WHAT'S TRACY PLAYING AT? THIS MOUSE ISN'T MY TYPE AT ALL!

OH, HI, LEE.

OH, THERE'S THE DOORBELL AGAIN, BYE!

I'LL KILL HER FOR THIS!

THIS IS AWFUL! WHAT ON EARTH AM I GOING TO SAY TO HIM?

SO WHAT DO YOU DO THEN, ER— SUSY?

REALLY?

OH, I'M—I'M STILL AT SCHOOL.

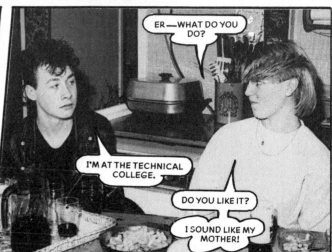

ER—WHAT DO YOU DO?

I'M AT THE TECHNICAL COLLEGE.

DO YOU LIKE IT?

I SOUND LIKE MY MOTHER!

YEAH, THEY'VE GOT GREAT SPORTS FACILITIES. I PLAY A LOT OF TENNIS THERE.

OH, I LOVE TENNIS! I'M A MEMBER OF GREENLANDS TENNIS CLUB!

REALLY? HOW GOOD ARE YOU?

Meanwhile . . .

GLAD YOU COULD MAKE IT, FAY.

DIDN'T WANT TO DISAPPOINT ALL THE FELLAS, DID I? HAPPY BIRTHDAY!

IS ALAN CLARK HERE? I'VE HEARD HE'S SPLIT UP WITH PAMELA GREAVES.

I DON'T KNOW. MY BROTHER'S INVITED LOADS OF HIS MATES. ALAN COULD BE WITH THEM. HAVE A LOOK AROUND.

And, in the kitchen . . .

I LOST THE SECOND SET BADLY, THOUGH.

WHAT HAPPENED? DID YOU LOSE YOUR CONCENTRATION?

SHE NOT BAD-LOOKING WHEN SHE SMILES!

53

I WONDER IF ALAN'S IN HERE?

HELLO!

SHE'S GORGEOUS!

SORRY — I WAS JUST LOOKING FOR SOMEONE.

HOLD ON. MAYBE I CAN HELP YOU!

And . . .

OH, WELL, SO MUCH FOR THE POWER OF PERSONALITY OVER BEAUTY! STILL, I'M NOT TOO HEARTBROKEN. HE WAS A BIT FLASH FOR ME!

And, at the door . . .

OH, HI, VIC. DANNY SAID YOU WERE COMING. GRAB A DRINK AND CIRCULATE!

OH — ER — GREAT!

I'LL HEAD FOR THE KITCHEN — THERE WON'T BE ANYONE IN THERE.

OH — ER — I DIDN'T EXPECT ANYONE — I MEAN — MOST PEOPLE ARE DANCING . . .

IS HE ASKING ME TO DANCE OR NOT? HE'S NICE!

I DON'T REALLY LIKE DANCING THAT MUCH . . .

I WISH HE'D SAY SOMETHING OR GO AWAY!

SPEAK TO HER, YOU FOOL! DON'T LOSE THIS CHANCE!

ER — SEE YOU, THEN!

I DON'T KNOW WHY I BOTHER COMING TO PARTIES! I ALWAYS MAKE A FOOL OF MYSELF. THAT GIRL IN THE KITCHEN LOOKED NICE, TOO.

54

THIS IS THE WORST PARTY I'VE EVER BEEN TO! ALAN'S NOT HERE AND I JUST CAN'T GET AWAY FROM THAT CREEP, LEE! HE'S AWFUL! I'M GOING TO HAVE TO LATCH ON TO ANOTHER BLOKE — AND FAST! AH, HE LOOKS QUITE SHY!

HELLO, DON'T MIND IF I SIT NEXT TO YOU, DO YOU?

ER — NO — I DON'T MIND!

OH NO, I HATE PUSHY GIRLS LIKE THIS! TOO MUCH MAKE-UP AND ENOUGH PERFUME TO START A FACTORY!

I WONDER WHERE FAY'S GOT TO? SHE WAS SUPPOSED TO BE GETTING A DRINK FROM THE KITCHEN, BUT THAT WAS TWENTY MINUTES AGO!

But . . .

I'VE ALWAYS LIKED THE IDEA OF WORKING WITH ANIMALS.

REALLY?

HE'S QUITE GOOD-LOOKING IN A FUNNY SORT OF WAY! FRIENDLY, TOO! HE'S REALLY QUITE NICE!

OH HI, LEE. THIS IS VIC!

OK, I GET THE MESSAGE!

I'LL SEE YOU LATER, THEN!

ALL ON YOUR OWN? COME AND DANCE!

MM, GLAMOUR GIRL MUST HAVE DITCHED HIM! I MAY BE SHY BUT I'M NOT STUPID!

NO THANKS, LEE. I DON'T LIKE DANCING MUCH.

WHAT'S THE MATTER? WHY DOESN'T SHE FANCY ME?

LOOK, I'LL GET TRACY TO PUT ON A SLOW RECORD — THERE'S NOT A LOT OF DANCING TO DO THEN! I'LL BE BACK IN A MINUTE!

THERE'S NO WAY I'M GOING TO DANCE WITH THAT CREEP! I'LL HIDE IN THE CUPBOARD!

And . . .

I JUST CAN'T GET AWAY FROM THAT MANEATER! I'LL HIDE IN THAT CUPBOARD UNTIL SHE GETS HER CLAWS INTO SOMEONE ELSE!

OK, SUSY, THERE'S A SLOW RECORD ON NOW! HEY, WHERE'S SHE GONE?

VIC, WHERE ARE YOU?

I THINK WE'LL STAY IN HERE AND LET THEM FIGHT IT OUT! WHAT DO YOU THINK?

I AGREE, I THINK THIS PARTY'S GOING TO BE GOOD FUN!

THE END 55

Continued from page 51

Even if you haven't found a complete band, the next thing to do is either write or choose songs that you'd like to perform.

Cover versions of other people's material are quite common among most new band's performances. It's always quite a big kick to be able to play a song that you've always liked, but be careful, because very few bands become successful by playing only old Roxy Music numbers!

Writing songs is not as difficult as you would probably first imagine, but writing *good* ones unfortunately is. There are so many techniques used by people who write their own material that it's practically impossible to say, "This is how you can write a song"!

Two methods which are quite common however are:-

a. **JAMMING:** Get yourself and the rest of the band in a room and just throw ideas around in the air. Maybe your drummer will start playing a rhythm which inspires the bass player to begin playing.

Song structures are often loosely arranged this way.

b. **SKETCHING:** If you are the vocalist or the person who writes the vocal melodies in the band, then chances are you have already tried this method.

Sit at home with a piece of paper and a pen and *write* a song! Just sing something that you think sounds good and write something you can sit and sing.

Then you can take this to your guitarist or keyboards player, find out the chord progression that you're singing. You can then arrange what the other instruments are going to play after that.

IMPORTANT: You'll probably find that if you're trying to play *pop* music it's quite important for at least *one* member of the band to be quite experienced musically.

HOW DO I GET TO THE TOP?

These days it's quite important for one member of the band to keep an eye on what's happening as far as the business side of things goes.

There are many different ways of making it to the top:

a. **BUILDING UP A FOLLOWING**

This is the most traditional way of going about trying to become a star. The simple fact is that you must play lots of gigs, build up quite an amount of provincial 'fans' of your band, and then hope that you get spotted.

This is by no stretch of imagination the best way of making it big.

b. **SELF-PROMOTION**

It's essential that you take your band into a recording studio as soon as you feel you're competent to work under those circumstances. Having a good tape of your band is one of the essential aspects of self-promotion.

Some bands use their studio tapes as a product which they sell by mail order but others simply send their tapes to record companies, radio stations and discos.

It also helps if your band also enclose black and white or colour photos (image *is* very important!) and a short biography of how your band got together and what they want to do.

AGENTS AND MANAGERS

You must realise that the music business *is* a business and that there'll be a lot of people who are trying to make money out of your band.

It's very difficult to explain how you should approach agents or managers, mainly because you can't predict how they're going to react. However, they can be essential to a fledgling band . . .

Finally, the music business *isn't* as glamorous as you may be led to believe. Chances are if you get to the stage where you're trying to *sell* your band, then you'll be in for lots of disappointments, but you *will* keep trying if you believe enough in yourself and your chance of stardom.

Look at all the other girls who have managed to make it in the music business!

Please keep in touch with Patches—we can help as well!

Good luck!

OK– SO YOU'RE BORED

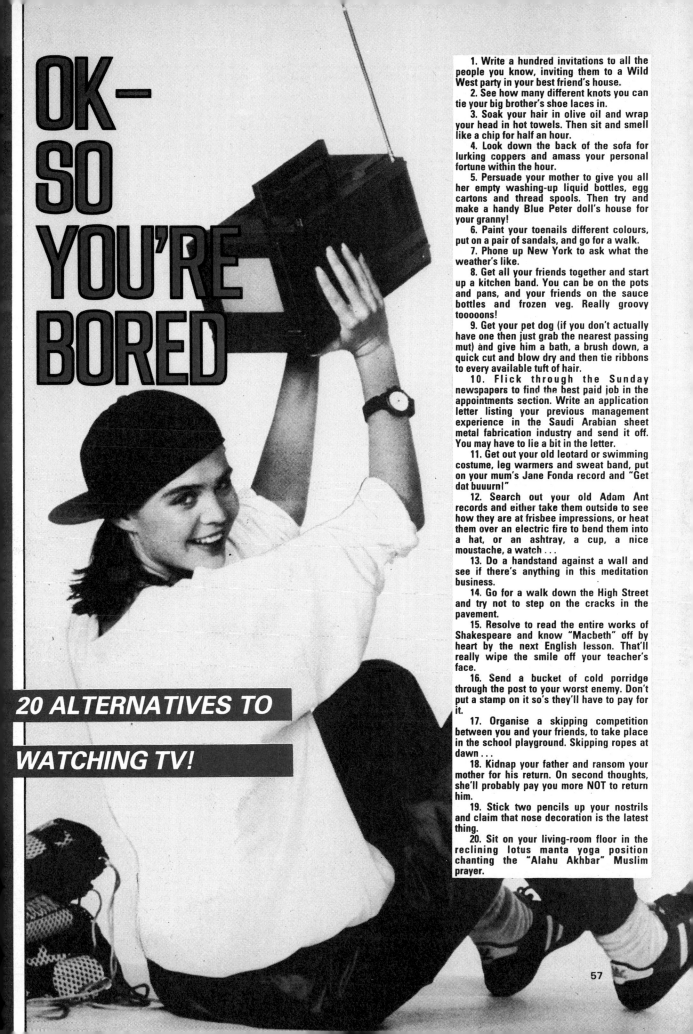

20 ALTERNATIVES TO WATCHING TV!

1. Write a hundred invitations to all the people you know, inviting them to a Wild West party in your best friend's house.

2. See how many different knots you can tie your big brother's shoe laces in.

3. Soak your hair in olive oil and wrap your head in hot towels. Then sit and smell like a chip for half an hour.

4. Look down the back of the sofa for lurking coppers and amass your personal fortune within the hour.

5. Persuade your mother to give you all her empty washing-up liquid bottles, egg cartons and thread spools. Then try and make a handy Blue Peter doll's house for your granny!

6. Paint your toenails different colours, put on a pair of sandals, and go for a walk.

7. Phone up New York to ask what the weather's like.

8. Get all your friends together and start up a kitchen band. You can be on the pots and pans, and your friends on the sauce bottles and frozen veg. Really groovy tooooons!

9. Get your pet dog (if you don't actually have one then just grab the nearest passing mut) and give him a bath, a brush down, a quick cut and blow dry and then tie ribbons to every available tuft of hair.

10. Flick through the Sunday newspapers to find the best paid job in the appointments section. Write an application letter listing your previous management experience in the Saudi Arabian sheet metal fabrication industry and send it off. You may have to lie a bit in the letter.

11. Get out your old leotard or swimming costume, leg warmers and sweat band, put on your mum's Jane Fonda record and "Get dot buuurn!"

12. Search out your old Adam Ant records and either take them outside to see how they are at frisbee impressions, or heat them over an electric fire to bend them into a hat, or an ashtray, a cup, a nice moustache, a watch . . .

13. Do a handstand against a wall and see if there's anything in this meditation business.

14. Go for a walk down the High Street and try not to step on the cracks in the pavement.

15. Resolve to read the entire works of Shakespeare and know "Macbeth" off by heart by the next English lesson. That'll really wipe the smile off your teacher's face.

16. Send a bucket of cold porridge through the post to your worst enemy. Don't put a stamp on it so's they'll have to pay for it.

17. Organise a skipping competition between you and your friends, to take place in the school playground. Skipping ropes at dawn . . .

18. Kidnap your father and ransom your mother for his return. On second thoughts, she'll probably pay you more NOT to return him.

19. Stick two pencils up your nostrils and claim that nose decoration is the latest thing.

20. Sit on your living-room floor in the reclining lotus manta yoga position chanting the "Alahu Akhbar" Muslim prayer.

A ROSE FOR LOVE

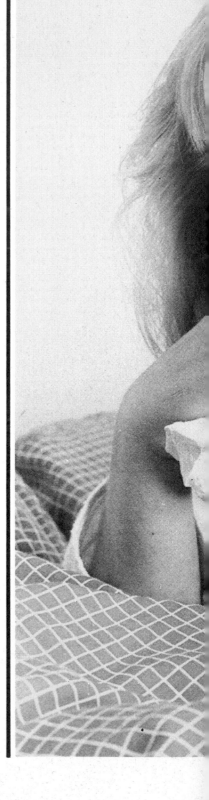

"I don't want to see you ever again!" I'd told him. So what was I doing now, waiting for him to come home?

THE rose had started to droop. I sat clutching it, staring dismally at its withering petals. All around me in the bustling, cold, damp station, people shoved. Recorded carols belted out, and the tinsel on the lonely Christmas tree flickered in the dirty yellow lights.

The nasal tones of the station announcer bleeped through "Good King Wenceslas" to announce that the 1.13 from Glasgow, due to arrive at 5.45, would arrive shortly at platform four. My heart lurched and the rose trembled in my hands. The station clock crept towards half-past nine, and the announcer apologised for the delay.

"Well!" I muttered to the sad rose. "This is it! He's arriving soon."

Some dishevelled drunk with a skewed tie stared at me and laughed, "Happy Christmas to you, too! It's a good party, isn't it?"

I tried to smile as I edged away. I'd been moving away from the drunken remains of office parties for nearly four hours. I was tired and cold and trembling with something that could have been tiredness, or could have been cold, but was probably nerves.

"Don't know why you bothered, Eve! You told him you'd finished with him. You told him you never wanted to see his silly grinning face again, ever. So what're you doing waiting for him?"

I didn't have an answer to that one.

He'd gone away to college last September and I'd put an end to all the stupidity there was between us.

"I don't want to write, and I don't want to phone, and I don't want to see you ever again!" I'd said.

Mum had more or less pushed me into it. She said it wasn't fair to hold on to him, and I ought to let him enjoy himself at college. And anyway, she said, I'd probably meet someone else on my course at the Tech.

I had. I'd met Janie and Alison and Collette. There weren't many boys taking the Typing and Secretarial Skills Certificate, except Nigel, and he didn't really count, because he'd made it clear that he wasn't interested from the start. I'd met several different guys at Tech. discos, and I'd also had a few dates with Janie's cousin, Lewis, who wore open-necked shirts, medallions and was prone to chest-colds. Oh, and the postman had winked at me, twice.

"You're not even trying to find a replacement for John," Mum had groaned at me finally. "What am I going to do with you? His mother said he's arriving home on the sixteenth, if you're interested!"

"What time?" I'd enquired, casually, trying to look as if I couldn't care less, even though my heart was performing somersaults.

"Early evening, she said."

I hadn't fooled Mum one little bit when I'd telephoned this afternoon, to say I wouldn't be home till late, because I was going out with Janie, Collette and Alison to celebrate the end of term.

"OK, dear," she'd said. "But just . . . just don't get your hopes up, Eve. He's probably found someone else by now."

58

"Who's probably found someone else by now?" I had asked, pretending total innocence.

"Oh! Father Christmas!" she had yelled, and slammed the phone down.

I'd bought my rose, I'd put on some fresh make-up, and I'd drunk seven cups of tea, alone. I couldn't force food into the churning emptiness that used to be my stomach. I'd just waited while the train ran into avalanches and blizzards, listened to every report about the delays, and wondered what I'd say. More to the point, I wondered what *he'd* say, or do, or not do, when he saw me and my forlorn rose, my desperate little smile, and my heart on my sleeve.

I tried to hide myself in the crowd at the barrier to watch the rush from the delayed train. It's difficult when you're five foot eight, clutching a red rose and wearing a nose to match, but I didn't want him to see me before I caught sight of him. I'd be able to tell, as soon as I saw that funny lop-sided face and the grin, whether it could still work miracles, or whether I'd been fooling myself about being crazily in love with him all this time.

If it didn't work, if my heart didn't flip and my toes didn't tingle and if I didn't catch that grin, I could disappear into the background and mingle with the drunks and the Christmas tree, and he'd be none the wiser.

"I know you, don't I? Aren't you Rudolf the Red Nosed Reindeer?" a very familiar husky voice whispered in my ear. I turned towards the grin that I'd missed so much. And there was the flip, and the tingle, as always.

"John! I . . ." I began to stammer, ready to hurl myself into his arms. But that position was already taken. A dark, curly-haired girl, small and beautiful, wearing dark-tinted glasses and looking like a refugee from an Italian movie, was already there. Mum was right. Someone else.

"Eve, meet Hazel." He smiled, and turned to her. "Hazel, this very tall voice you'll hear in a minute is coming from a broomstick that I used to be very, very friendly with."

"Hi!" I squeaked, hiding the rose behind my back, holding out my hand and sniffing. But the tear fell down my cheek just the same. Hazel ignored my hand. She just smiled.

"Hi!" she said brightly. "John's been very kind to me. He's just going to see me on to the next train, my London connection. I hope you don't mind?"

"No!" I said sheepishly. I had seen the white stick she carried, and knew that there was no threat here, in John helping a stranger, a blind girl, from a train.

"I'll carry your case!" I told her, sliding round to the other side of the most fantastic boy in the world, the boy I just couldn't stop loving.

"Hey, Eve," he whispered to me, giving me the wink that said it was the same for him, too. "They're playing our song!"

And as we walked towards the London train on platform two, the tannoy blared "Comfort and Joy."

"Happy Christmas and welcome home," I murmured, fitting one very battered, but proud, red rose into a buttonhole of his leather jacket.

59

WHAT TO DO WITH AN OLD  BAG...

Here we give you part 73 in our series of tips on making some Chic on the Cheap, creating Flash without Cash. Well . . . let's say we're going to show you some use for the useless.

Once you've savoured the flavour, how many times have you sat playing with an empty crisp bag, folding it into all sorts of interesting shapes or simply crushing it in your hand before throwing it on to a table and watching it unfold? Never! Then you've been missing out. But we're here to help.

From the mountain of empty packets left behind at the end of a day in the Patches office we've come up with the following ideas:

1. The Child Detector. It must have happened to you. You've waited for weeks to be on your own with that dishy fella. Finally the moment comes. You're babysitting and the little horrors are tucked-up in bed. At last, alone together on the living room sofa, gentle music playing in the background, he puts his arm around your shoulder and leans forward. Then, just as your lips are about to meet, the door opens and a little voice whines, "Can I have a drink of water?" The moment has gone and the evening spoiled.

Such an embarrassing moment can be avoided by crushing empty crisp bags and

scattering them around outside the door. The noise made as the little angel walks across them should give you plenty of warning.

Remember. The empty bag is the important bit for you. Crisps have no regard for the figure of the person eating them, so it might be a good idea to let the brats scoff them before you send them to bed. They also serve as handy bribes.

2. A Bow For Your Beau. Smarten up the boy in your life—make him a bow tie! Simply fold your crisp bag in half three times, from side to side so that you have a long thin strip of brightly coloured cellophane, then tie a knot in the middle of it and you have it!

Remember. It's important to choose the flavour carefully, the colour of the bag must go with his best shirt and the lingering scent of Sweet and Sour Tadpole mustn't clash with his aftershave.

If you want him to look as smooth as Andrew Ridgeley of Wham, make him a "Western Style" bow tie. Follow the above instructions then thread a second bag through the knot and pull it down the way. You may have to sit on this one for a while to make sure it's flat enough. To attach the bow to your beloved's neck, simply thread a ribbon through the knot and put it around under his collar. How tightly you tie it depends on what he thinks of the pressie!

3. A Pet Parachute. If your frog has perfected the upward flight in his jump but hasn't quite mastered the downward stage, or perhaps the hamster gets over-excited on his little wheel and sends himself into orbit, then this is the answer for you! Blow your bag up like a balloon. Make two loops with thread for his arms to go through and attach them to the bag with sticky tape.

Remember. Check your pet's health with a vet before trying these exercises.

So what of the rest of our suggestions? Pay attention, these involve some dexterous origami (don't worry, you won't get into trouble for it—origami is the ancient oriental art of paper folding). For the sake of your sanity it's best to follow the steps in our illustration before you go any further.

Hmm! You'll now either have a neat triangle or be back at idea one! Once you've mastered the shape it can be used as:

4. A brightly coloured tip for that dull old tie.

5. An earring. Simply push your lobe into the space between the front and the back. This one works best with a thick ear—perhaps your mum will help you!

6. A protector for the rubber on the end of your pencil.

7. Covers for the toes on your most pointed shoes.

8. False fingernails (you need ten for this—just to save you counting).

9. A high-tech pop badge. By adding your own safety pin, wear it as you like, or add any number together by pushing the point of one triangle into the opening of another to make a bigger badge.

10. A bookmark. Simply slide it on to the corner of the page you are at.

With a little thought, we're sure you'll come up with lots more ideas. Probably they'll be a lot more useful!

And no, our next tip won't be on how to make a super squeezy bottle from an old space shuttle—Blue Peter beat us to that.

ACTION MAN

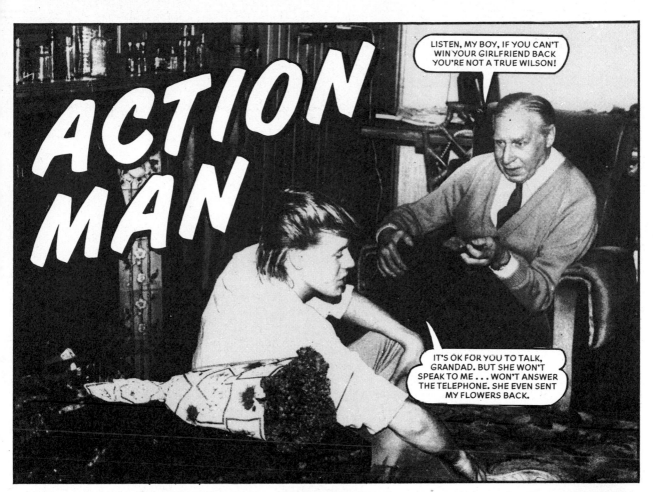

61

"A few days later I learned that Stanley was taking Lucy to the Grand Charity Ball . . ."

HE'S NOT GOING TO GET AWAY WITH IT!

"On the night of the ball . . ."

OOO-WOOOBY-DOO!

HAH! I'LL NAB 'EM IN THE MIDDLE OF THE CHARLESTON!

WAAAOOOH! PUT ME DOWN! YOU OAF! YOU MANIAC!

YOU'RE MY GIRL AND WE'RE LEAVING!

"When we got outside . . ."

SORRY ABOUT THAT. BUT I . . .

OH, TED. MY VALENTINO! MY HERO!

"Believe me, Steven, it paid off . . ."

I was impressed . . .

I DIDN'T THINK THAT MACHO STUFF WORKED. I'LL HAVE TO GIVE IT A TRY!

OF COURSE YOU WILL! YOU'RE A WILSON, AREN'T YOU? FOLLOW IN MY FOOTSTEPS, LAD.

Later . . .

SEE YOU THEN! KEEP YOUR FINGERS CROSSED SHE'S THERE.

GOOD LUCK, LAD. ALTHOUGH YOU DON'T NEED IT!

But, as Grandad dozed off . . .

TCH! TCH! YOU SHOULD BE ASHAMED, TED WILSON — TELLING STEVE THAT OLD STORY. YOU KNOW IT'S ONLY HALF TRUE.

AH, LEAVE ME BE, LUCY. CAN'T YOU SEE I'M TRYING TO GET SOME SHUT-EYE?

YOU SHOULD HAVE TOLD HIM THE TRUTH!

"What really happened was . . ."

PUF, PHEW! WHEE . . . I DIDN'T REALISE YOU WERE THIS HEAVY!

PUT ME DOWN, YOU IDIOT!

"They caught up with you outside . . ."

INTO THE FOUNTAIN WITH HIM!

AAAGH!!

SHALL WE GO BACK INSIDE, LUCY?

ER . . . WELL, I DON'T THINK SO, STANLEY. I'D BETTER GO AND HELP TED.

MY HERO! MY VALENTINO! HOW STRONG! HOW MASTERFUL!

SH . . . SH . . . SHUT UP, LUCY! GIVE ME YOUR SHAWL BEFORE I CATCH PNEUMONIA.

"But we did kiss and make up . . ."

I JUST HOPE STEVE WON'T BE AS STUPID AS YOU! HE MIGHT GET INTO A FIGHT.

UH . . . ER . . . WELL, MAYBE I DID LAY IT ON A BIT THICK. BUT HE'LL BE OK. DON'T WORRY, DEAR.

Meanwhile . . .

I'LL GO STRAIGHT IN TO THE PARTY . . . SWEEP ALISON OFF HER FEET! JUST LIKE GRANDAD!

But she'd met someone else . . .

AH . . . ER . . . WELL, HE'S BUILT LIKE DALEY THOMSON . . .

THAT'S HER EX. WHAT'S HE STARING AT?

Discretion was definitely the better part of valour . . .

I PROBABLY LEAN MORE TO THE COWARDLY SIDE OF THE FAMILY. GRANDAD WOULD BE ASHAMED OF ME, BUT I'M TOO YOUNG TO COMMIT SUICIDE!

63

You may not know it, but the changes in weather take their toll on your skin. Winter is the time when you're especially prone to dry skin, chapped lips, watery eyes and a bright red nose! So, if you don't want to spend Christmas masquerading as Rudolf, read on!

LET'S GLOW FOR IT!

YOU can get away with very little skin care in summer, because a tan covers up a multitude of sins, and everyone looks good. Winter beauty, however, needs a lot more attention, and it's vital that you keep your skin well moisturised.

Think of all the punishment your face is taking—the cold wind that blows in your eyes and the sudden changes from freezing temperatures to centrally heated schools and offices. Try carrying around your favourite moisturiser with you, and smoothing in a tiny drop every few hours or so. This will also help prevent those red cheeks that leave your skin feeling sore.

Take extra care with your normal cleansing routine, too. Try using a more gentle cleanser and toner, like Ten-O-Six Deep-Pore Cleanser for dry, sensitive skin by Bonne Bell. It's strong enough to take away the grime, but gentle enough not to do any harm to skin that's already dry. Try smoothing on E45 cream last thing at night, too. It's a non-greasy moisturiser that also has no perfumes to irritate sensitive skin—perfect for the winter!

If you find that you simply can't get rid of those red cheeks, try using Boots No. 7 Colour Corrective moisturiser. It contains a pale green tint which cools down the redness and covers imperfections. Or why not cheat and carry that summer tan right through the winter? Coty's Sunshimmer applied with a damp sponge gives a glowing natural look—and perhaps looking healthy will fool all these winter 'flu and cold germs!

Chapped lips and possible cold sores are another two winter miseries. Using lip salve or a dab of Vaseline every few hours will help, but if you've left it too late and your lips are cracked and sore then you need Blisteze Cream. It has a pleasant wintergreen taste and can also be used on cold sores. You'll have to ask for it at the chemist counter, though, as it *is* medicated.

Spots are a problem all year round, but in winter you tend to slow down and your system becomes sluggish, which in turn can cause more spots. It takes a determined effort to force yourself into doing some sort of exercise to pep up your circulation and so prevent bad skin. Why not do a few, quick, stretching exercises to your favourite record every night? It's better than nothing—and it might help burn off the heavy food we tend to eat in winter.

Watch what you're eating! Too much stodge and greasy food can give you an unhealthy grey pallor as well as blemishes. Your body does need more food—to burn as heat—in the cold weather, but don't make that an excuse to dive into the chocs and chips. Reach for an apple if you can't survive as far as the next meal—it's better for you.

Backs and shoulders are especially greasy and prone to spots, because we're all so well wrapped up in winter and those big heavy jumpers cause your skin to sweat. The way to fight this is to keep yourself extra clean. Scrub your back with a loofah and a deodorant soap, and rub on some toner on a cotton wool pad last thing at night.

Make-up doesn't have to be specially for winter, but you may feel that you want a change from the colours you wore all summer. Be careful what type of mascara you use—cold winds can cause eyes to water and make eye make-up run, so your best bet is a waterproof mascara.

So, cheer up—winter isn't all that bad! Just think of all those Christmas and New Year parties you're going to dazzle everyone at now that you've followed our advice. Enjoy yourself!

D'you rate Christmas as the brightest time of year or has its sparkle gone? Let our fun quiz find out if you'd make it as one of Santa's elves!

WHAT SANTA HAVE YOU GOT YOUR CLAUS INTO?

Little things can tell a great deal about the kind of person you really are. How you act in certain circumstances, and what you do, can give enormous clues about the kind of bloke you'd be happiest with.

Don't believe us?

Well, this quiz has all the answers. Try it!

1. JUST AS A GUIDELINE, WHEN DO YOU USUALLY START THINKING ABOUT DOING YOUR CHRISTMAS SHOPPING?
a) As soon as the summer sales start.
b) About the end of November.
c) Your mum arranges things for you.
d) What shopping?

2. YOU'RE IN A LARGE STORE WHEN YOU PASS SANTA'S GROTTO. DO YOU:
b) wish you were six again and could go and sit on his knee,
d) go and sit on his knee and tug his beard,
a) ignore him — you never believed in him anyway,
c) look forward to when you'll have kids of your own to take?

3. YOU'VE JUST BUST UP WITH YOUR BOYFRIEND. YOU HADN'T BOUGHT HIM A PRESSIE. DO YOU:
c) buy him one anyway — it *is* Christmas after all,
a) feel relieved. It means you can get that dress you wanted,
b) send him a card — no hard feelings,
d) get a T-shirt printed with 'HAPPY CHRISTMAS, CREEP' and leave it on his doorstep?

4. YOU'VE BEEN LAST MINUTE SHOPPING, YOU'RE TIRED, YOUR HEAD HURTS, AND YOU'VE JUST MISSED THE BUS. SUDDENLY IT STARTS TO SNOW HEAVILY. DO YOU:
d) start skipping and singing 'White Christmas',
b) grin and feel a bit better— maybe the hassle's worth it after all,
a) hail a taxi — no point in getting wet,
c) wish you were hand-in-hand with a dishy snowman?

5. HOW D'YOU LIKE TO SPEND CHRISTMAS EVE?
a) At the disco with your mates.
b) At home with your family and fella.
c) Carol singing at an old folk's home.
d) Organising an on-the-spot party?

6. IT'S CHRISTMAS MORNING. WHAT D'YOU DO FIRST?
c) Look out the window in case it's snowed overnight.
d) Yell, 'Yippee!' and rush around waking up the entire house.
a) Take your mum and dad breakfast in bed.
b) Make a pile of all your presents — savouring the opening until everybody else is up.

7. YOUR BOYFRIEND GAVE YOU A BULKY, GIFT-WRAPPED PRESENT ON CHRISTMAS EVE. WHEN YOU OPEN IT, IS IT:
a) thermal underwear,
b) exactly what you've always wanted (although you hadn't realised it before),
c) a gallon of your favourite perfume,
d) a box of indoor fireworks and a Christmas stocking full of games and sweets?

8. AFTER THE BIG MEAL, WHAT DO YOU DO WITH THE REST OF THE DAY?
b) Flake out in front of the telly.
d) Organise a snowball fight, even if there isn't any snow.
a) Go for a long brisk walk to work off the food.
c) Sit in your room, daydreaming.

9. YOU CAN GO ANYWHERE IN THE WORLD FOR CHRISTMAS. DO YOU CHOOSE:
d) Lapland — Santa has to be somewhere!
c) Vienna — waltzing in the snow,
b) Home — it's where your heart is,
a) Australia — you can't stand the cold and wet?

10. WHEN YOUR FELLA VISITS ON CHRISTMAS DAY, WHAT'S THE FIRST THING YOU DO?
a) Wish him 'Happy Christmas' and give him his present.
b) Give him a huge hug and a kiss.
c) Breathlessly tell him you thought tonight would never come.
d) Ask him to plug in the fairy lights on your dress.

WELL, WHAT D'YOU RECKON? ARE YOU A CHRISTMAS CRACKER OR A DAMP SQUIB?
ADD UP YOUR SCORE — MOSTLY A's, B's, C's OR D's — THEN TAKE A LOOK!

Mainly a's —
Practical and down-to-earth — your enemies might even call you 'boring'. You dislike taking chances, mainly because you tend to get a bit confused when you do, and you like to keep your own life very much in order. Your ideal other half would be someone similar, with a strong personality, and a strong sense of right and wrong. Hopefully, though, he'd also need to have a sense of humour and be able to make you laugh occasionally.

Mainly b's —
Ms Average — you're a mixture, like most of us. Your sensible and practical side is balanced by a soft heart although you'll never suffer fools gladly. You care about things and people, particularly your own family. You're at your happiest with the boy next door' — the shyer type of boy whom nobody else ever notices but who is full of hopes and dreams the same as yours. Keep a tight grip on him — he's worth his weight in gold.

Mainly c's —
You're a romantic, daydreaming optimist. As you tend to see the best in everything and everyone, you can be badly shaken and hurt when you're faced with their nastier sides. You desperately need a bloke you feel you can trust and lean on; someone who'll look after you and put you first in his life. When you find him, you'll care about him very deeply indeed, and do everything in your power to make him happy. But then, he'll be expected to do that for you, too!

Mainly d's —
It must be said that on the face of it, you're nothing but downright scatty! You charge into things without thinking twice. You've a daredevil attitude, you like fun and excitement, and can't bear sitting still. You'd make the ideal Christmas present for the kind of bloke who's pretty self-sufficient, but who likes taking a risk and having fun as much as you do. At any party, you are guaranteed to be the centre of attention — and so is he!

66

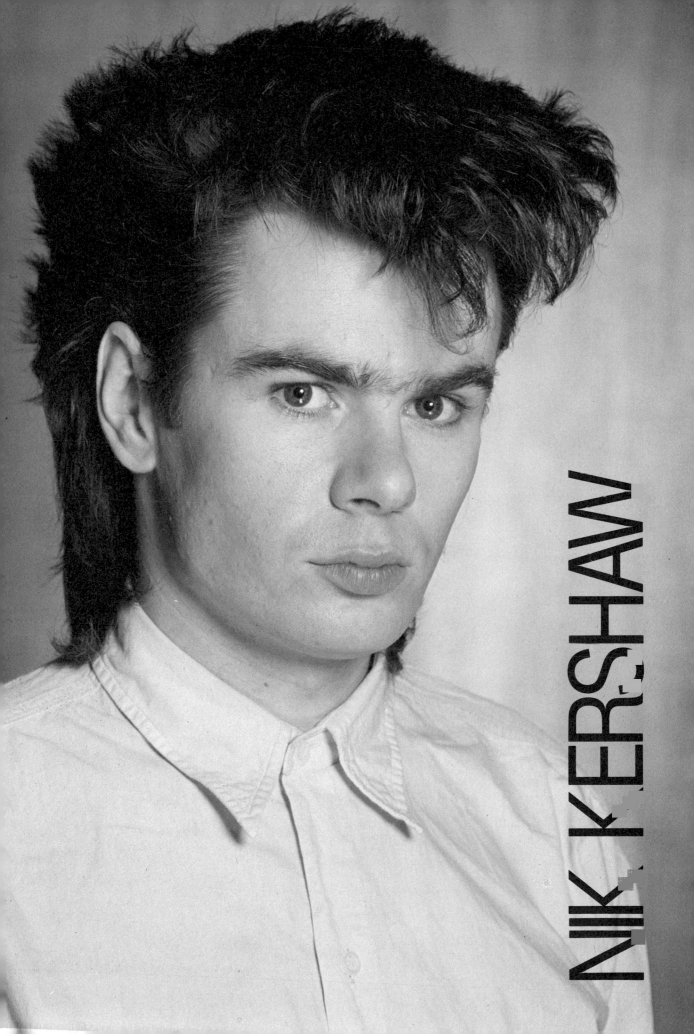

NIK KERSHAW

PopTeesers

Hiya, folks!

We here at PopTeesers decided that all our readers were having far too much fun, so we decided to lay on loads and loads of daft pop questions for you to have a great time answering.

OK, I know there're no fivers up for grabs this time, but it'll sure give you lots of practice for when there are!

1. What is George Michael's nickname?
2. Who released an album called 'Human's Lib'?
3. Can you name King's first top ten hit?
4. Limahl had one of his biggest hits to-date with 'Never Ending Story'. Can you name the box office smash movie that it was featured in?
5. What's Prince's favourite colour?
6. Name the two brothers who are guitarist and bass player with Spandau Ballet.
7. What's Morrissey's favourite type of flower?
8. Where does Alison Moyet hail from originally?
9. What's the link between Frankie Goes to Hollywood, A.B.C., The Art of Noise and Malcolm McLaren?
10. What colour was Nick Rhodes' suit on his wedding day?
11. Which of the following pop stars isn't married. a) Howard Jones b) Nik Kershaw c) Jimi Somerville d) Alison Moyet?
12. Name the band that John and Andy Taylor from Duran formed with Robert Palmer.
13. Can you name the spotty Scotsman who sings with Aztec Camera?
14. Terry Hall sang with three bands. Name them.
15. What was The Jam's last single?
16. Can you remember what was last year's Christmas No.1?
17. Which movie did The Eurythmics provide the soundtrack for last year?
18. Name the gender bending vocalist with Dead Or Alive.

19. Hugh Cornwell and Jean Jaques Burnel are both in which band?
20. True Or False? Culture Club's first single reached No.1.
21. Name Paul Young's first two solo albums.
22. What is Suggs of Madness' real name?
23. Who were the two pop stars behind Tina Turner's comeback?
24. True Or False? Black Lace were once Britain's entry for the Eurovision Song contest.
25. What was the name of the single that Tears For Fears first burst onto the pop charts with?
26. Who writes the lyrics for The Thompson Twins' hits?
27. What's Sting's real name?
28. Which of these songs DIDN'T Status Quo record? a) The Wanderer b) The Riddle or c) Rockin' All Over The World.
29. Do you know what Boy George's real name is?
30. Can you name the mime artist who works with Howard Jones?
31. True Or False? When Divine first appeared on T.O.T.P., the B.B.C. switchboard was crammed with complaints.
32. Is Simon Le Bon a) 32 b) 27 c) 23?
33. What did Nick Rhodes call his first book of photographs?
34. What was the name of the last album that Japan recorded together?
35. True Or False? Tom Bailey was a teacher before he became a popstar.
36. True Or False? When Tony Blackburn was a naughty young lad, he was a D.J. for pirate station, Radio Caroline.
37. How long did it take for 'Relax' to reach No.1? Was it a)2 weeks b)3 months or c) 3 years?
38. Which member of Heaven 17 wasn't in The Human League?
39. What was the name of the movie that Madness made about their early days?
40. Name Nick Heyward's first solo single.
41. Which Billy Bragg song did Kirsty MacColl take into the charts?
42. True Or False? Nik Kershaw was once in a band called 'Half Pint Hog'.
43. Which of the following DOESN'T Morrissey list as his greatest heroes. a) Billy Fury b) Sandie Shaw or c) George Michael?
44. Name Bronski Beat's debut album.
45. What does Michael Jackson call his pet

boa constrictor?
46. Can you name Midge Ure's first solo single?
47. Who made the movie that The Smiths' first album cover was a still from?
48. Which film was Freddie Mercury's 'Love Kills' part of the soundtrack of?
49. Queen's drummer shares his name with another famous drummer. Which band does he play with?
50. Which legendary band recorded 'Love Is The Drug'?
51. Which of Culture Club's videos was (supposed!) to have been filmed on the banks of the Mississippi?
52. Did The Thompson Twins record their first album in a) Paris, b) London or c) the Bahamas?
53. Where do Echo And The Bunnymen come from?
54. What's David Bowie's real name?
55. Name the female vocalist who has worked with both The Style Council and Wham.
56. True Or False? Simon Le Bon used to drive a tractor for a living.
57. Which soul band did Paul Young front before he decided to go solo?
58. Which was the first single that Michael Jackson released from the 'Thriller' album?

59. Vox is the surname of which famous Irish frontman?
60. Which famous politician appeared in one of Tracey Ullman's videos?
61. True Or False? Marilyn lived in a squat in London with Boy George and Tom Bailey.
62. Name wee Lloyd Cole's first hit single.
63. Where did Duran Duran get their name?
64. Which of the following bands hasn't Malcolm McLaren managed. a) The Sex Pistols b) Frankie Goes To Hollywood c) Bow Wow Wow?
65. Name the lead singer with Iron Maiden.
66. What's the name of the band that Suggs and Carl from Madness formed? (CLUE: It was based around a famous cartoon strip character.)
67. Which Robert Palmer song did Rod Stewart record a cover version of?
68. What is Sade's surname?
69. Which band does Earl Falconer play with?
70. Did Elton John marry in a) 1983, b) 1984 or c) 1985?
71. Who is Marco Pirroni?
72. What are the names of two girls from The Human League?
73. Name Wham's first album.
74. Name Depeche Mode's record label.
75. Why did you bother answering all these daft pop questions in the first place?

ANSWERS

P·E·R·F·E·C·T·L·Y AWFUL!

top! Don't throw him away just because he's average . . . you'd have more problems
with your boy if he was perfect. Don't believe us? Read on and be surprised!

THE trouble with boys is that they're never as perfect as you want them to be. And when it comes to boyfriends there's always something to complain about! They're unromantic, unfaithful, scruffy, selfish and inconsiderate. (But hopefully not all at once!)

There must be Perfect Boyfriends out there somewhere . . . what'll they be like when you find them? Well we've looked around on your behalf and here they are . . .

● Mr Romance

Your dreams have come true, at last your life is filled with romance. Isn't it wonderful to have a boyfriend who showers you with gifts and love-poems?

But what happens when you're reduced to plonking priceless orchids into empty milk-bottles 'cos you've run out of vases, and your room's beginning to look like a flower show? Suddenly you're sick of the sight of red roses, and even the *thought* of another expensive box of chocs is enough to make you throw-up.

And you're becoming embarrassed when he calls you his "dearest heart" or "little lotus petal" and everyone falls about laughing. Could these be signs that the novelty is beginning to wear off? You can have too much of a good thing, and soon you're left longing for just one little harsh word or blunt home truth . . .

● Mr Faithful

Aren't you the lucky one to have a boyfriend who never flirts or makes you jealous! "It must be super to have such a faithful and reliable boyfriend," rave your mates. "He's really crazy about you!"

"Yes, isn't he?" you reply smugly. And it's true. He does only have eyes for you. In fact his large doleful eyes never leave your face as he gazes at you constantly, dribbling slightly at the corners of his mouth while he follows you around. Who could wish for a more perfect relationship than one where your every wish is his command?

Well actually, you might possibly find that such devotion gets just a little bit tiresome in the long run. What sort of conversation can you have when he's too busy drooling at you to talk? Euch! — think of his kisses! So if you want big eyes and faithfulness you'd be better off with a dog.

● Mr Dazzle

Congratulations, on finding a boyfriend you feel proud to be seen with! He never lets you down by looking scruffy or untidy, he never smells of motor-oil (or worse), he's perfect from his shining hair and gleaming teeth right down to his dazzling polished shoes.

Your mates envy you 'cos he's so fantastic looking but what's the use of having a boyfriend when he's only for looking at? So, no hugging — he can't have your grubby hands on his clothes; no kissing — you might smudge *his* make-up or get some of yours on his shirt, and anyway, it's unhygienic!

Unless your idea of a slap up meal is a bowl of salad and some fruit juice (must take care of *his* figure) then give him a miss.

A human Toothpaste Advertisement isn't the answer to your prayers after all. Best let him go back to the magazines where he belongs!

● Mr Friendly

Phew! What a relief to have a boyfriend you can take home for tea without worrying what Mum and Dad are going to think. An end to all the rows and aggravations, all the complaints and criticisms? Well, your boyfriend will be greeted like a long lost son as soon as he steps in the doorway.

"Thank goodness she's found a *nice* boyfriend at last," sighs Mum. "He seems a really decent sort of chap," agrees Dad.

It's all hunky-dory and cosy chats round the tea-pot for the three of them, but what about you?

"Er — um —" you interrupt three hours later, "er, isn't it about time we set off for the disco, Nigel?"

But he's far too busy admiring Mum's holiday snaps of Wally Land to hear.

"Um —" you venture after another few hours. "Um, Nigel, don't you think it's about time we —?"

But, too late, he's now involved in a discussion with Dad about rotary lawnmowers and car-battery extension leads.

"Nigel, what about the —" you whisper in desperation, "— the disco . . .?"

When this happens there's nothing for it but to sneak off for the last five minutes of the disco on your own. Ah well, another beautiful relationship hits the dust — but at least Mum and Dad have a new friend! He'll probably get on well with your gran too!

● Mr Macho

Who cares about women's lib when you can have a manly hero of your very own?

Everywhere you go, he runs ahead flinging doors open for you, and if the door's locked, he'll rip it off its hinges no trouble at all. You never have to nag to get taken to the cinema, 'cos he's fixed up a schedule of entertainment three months in advance to save you having to think.

You fancy wild strawberries at midnight, or a Chinese take-away for breakfast? Never fear, Macho Man will zoom off into the night to perform miraculous deeds and impossible tasks — all for helpless you!

What *you* have to do (you lucky thing) is laze around looking pretty and being his idea of *female*. But, incredible though it may seem, it isn't *always* so super having superman as a boyfriend.

F'r instance, what'll you do when your arm muscles begin to waste away through never being allowed to lift a finger? Your brain is turning to porridge through not having to think for yourself. In the end, there's only one answer to the problem — use your power to make him vanish before he turns *you* into a vegetable!

● The Perfect Beast

Aagh! How did you manage to find such a monster of a boyfriend? He's useless, lazy, unreliable, moody, selfish, difficult, unpredictable, quick-tempered, unco-operative and inconsiderate. Why on earth do you put up with him?

Well . . . Perhaps it's just because he's human, and you love him for all his faults and failings! It's his bad qualities that make you appreciate his good ones more, and even the bad things about him give him character.

He rates as the Perfect Boyfriend because he has something all the others lack — he's a REAL PERSON . . . Mr Right?

BREAKDANCING

WHO: Almost everyone who managed to sneak past the doorman at the local A.B.C. to see "Flashdance" and "Beat Street" has tried it. You need a very strong neck and an ability to suffer pain.

WHERE: If you're hip, you dance on a piece of kitchen lino laid out of the pavement, or in busy shopping centres on a Saturday afternoon, so you'll get stared at. If you're unhip, you do it at the youth club, where everyone will laugh at you.

CLOTHES: Tracksuits (the older and scruffier the better) training shoes, baseball caps, thick gloves and zip-up nylon kagouls.

MUSIC: Basically, a collection of computerised bleeps punctuated by shrieks, heavy breathing and long "raps" (talking very fast, completely out of time with the music).

DANCE: Not so much dancing as rolling about on the floor, punctuated by a few amazing feats of acrobatics. Severe risk of broken necks, legs, arms etc.

If you're reading this Annual, you must be pretty stylish, right? Well, just to check, run your eye down this list and if you've ever done any of these dances—your street cred rating is 0!

The Patches Guide

HEADBANGING

WHO: Long-haired youths with big, powerful motorbikes and big, powerful girlfriends.

WHERE: Discos at the local motorcycling club, where the sound system keeps breaking down and the lights don't work properly. Also, very loud rock concerts.

CLOTHES: If they have motorbikes (they all dream of owning a 900 Kawasaki), they wear huge leather jackets with studs and fringes. If they don't, they wear jeans and denim jackets. The girls dress the same way as the boys and because the boys have long hair too, it's often difficult to tell them apart.

MUSIC: Very noisy, with guitars and drums banging away in the background while a long-haired person, sweating profusely, screams over the top of it all.

DANCE: The feet stay still and the "dancers" throw their heads from front to back and side to side, hair flying everywhere, while strumming imaginary guitars.

BALLET

WHO: Podgy little seven-year-old girls in pink tights and tutus who're dreaming of stage school and seeing their name in lights. At fourteen, they change miraculously into slim, leggy beauties.

WHERE: Miss Crabtree's Dancing School which is a crumbling Victorian tenement block in the grottiest part of town.

CLOTHES: Cute little net skirts, Persil-white leotards and pale pink tights set off by a matching hairband.

MUSIC: Tinkly Beethoven played by an ancient ex-ballerina on an equally ancient piano.

DANCE: Very graceful with lots of running about on tiptoe, leaping into the air and holding impossible positions for at least quarter of an hour.

To NAFF DANCING

COUNTRY and WESTERN

WHO: Middle-aged, overweight, beer-swilling men who think they're John Wayne and have never quite grown up, plus their wives, children or embarrassed girlfriends.

WHERE: Grotty function rooms in run-down hotels in the middle of nowhere.

CLOTHES: Faded, fraying, flared jeans (always an unknown brand), plastic cowboy boots, nylon shirts with fringes everywhere and either a huge black leather belt with a silver buckle or a gun in a holster.

MUSIC: Three-piece band playing ancient Johnny Cash and Glen Campbell hits with a bit of Crystal Gale thrown in for good measure.

DANCE: Lots of stamping of feet, clapping of hands and skipping round in circles. Noisy and VERY energetic.

BELLYDANCING

WHO: Devotees of bellydancing fall into two main categories:

Class 1):Dusky eastern maidens.

Class 2):Overweight, middle-aged, suburban housewives who see it as a great way to get fit.

WHERE:

Class 1):Any common old garden sultan's palace.

Class 2):A draughty church hall with creaky floorboards and an equally creaky janitor who's always making excuses to come in so he can watch.

CLOTHES:

Class 1):Lengths of chiffon and a few stragetically-placed sequins.

Class 2):Brightly-coloured leotards and legwarmers which show off all the rolls of fat.

MUSIC:

Class 1):Tinkling bells and cymbals.

Class 2):Ancient Demis Roussos records (it's the closest they could get to Turkish records in Woolworths!). They don't really need music anyway, as it's drowned out by the dancers' groans of agony.

DANCE:

Class 1):Rotating the hips without moving the rest of the body.

Class 2):Much the same, but with lots of wobbling flesh, grunts, groans and creaking floorboards.

HOW TO HAVE AN ALTERNATIVE CHRISTMAS!

1. Take along your summer holiday photos everywhere you go. People will be so bored they'll make sure they avoid you — and that way you can't help but be noticed!

2. Look as miserable as sin. Everyone else is happy at Christmas . . .

3. Dye your hair green and spike it up, Christmas tree style. Then add tinsel, fairy lights, baubles . . .

4. Stand in the middle of your local disco and shout and gibber like a maniac. Everyone is sure to have noticed you by the time the bouncers arrive to throw you out!

5. Dress up as Santa Claus *all* the time. People will certainly notice you 'cos the crowds trying to give you their Christmas lists won't leave you alone.

6. Wear that skimpy T-shirt and shorts you wore in Spain during the summer. OK, you may freeze, but you'll certainly be different!

7. Put a notice board outside your house saying that if a certain S. Claus comes anywhere near, you'll prosecute for trespassing!

8. Wander round the shops on Christmas Eve with your last-minute pressie list — for 1986!

9. Sing "We're All Going On A Summer Holiday" when everyone else is singing "Silent Night."

10. Set up a stall outside your house with all the unwanted soap and talc gift sets you got. You may not be popular, but no-one will miss you!

11. Refuse to have anything to do with glitter, spray-on snow, Christmas tree decorations, wrapping paper, gift tags . . .

12. Switch *off* your TV when everyone else is watching "Butch Cassidy And The Sundance Kid" for the millionth time.

13. Go to school or work!

14. If you're a Smiths' fan, go around with a Christmas tree sticking out your back pocket!

If you want to be different from everyone else this Christmas, why not try some of these ideas— they'll certainly get you noticed . . .

15. Never mind decking the hall with boughs of holly . . . Try necking in the hall with Holly Johnson instead!

16. Do the Agadoo dance when everyone else is doing the Grand Old Duke Of York at the school dance.

17. Go everywhere with your Calorie counter and loudly add up everything that you, and everyone else, is eating.

18. Laugh loudly at your dad's pathetic jokes. No-one ever laughs at them so you're sure to be noticed!

The A-Z of GOING OUT WITH BOYS

ARROGANT—The type of boy you'll want to avoid. He'll show you off to his friends and call you his "bird". Likely to drop you as quickly as he picked you up.

BORED—What you'll be when he's away to his Great Auntie Maud's for the weekend, and you're playing gooseberry with your friends and all their guys at the local disco.

CUDDLES—When he pulls you towards him and gives you a great big bear hug. Any luck and you might escape with only a few broken ribs and a mouthful of hairy jumper!

DING-DONG—The sound that the doorbell makes to tell you that he's called to take you out and you're still deciding which dress to wear. Never mind that you've still to have a bath, wash and dry your hair, put on your make up . . . Still, he'll have fun with your 3-year-old brother and the dog, who doesn't like him.

ELBOW—When he tells you it's all over and he's met someone else. Still, there's plenty more fish in the sea, plenty more pebbles on the beach, and plenty more people to irritate you by saying things like that . . .

FIGHTS—Everyone has them. It's when he says he wants to go to the big match on Saturday but you'd much rather go and see the latest "weepie" at the cinema. And you both fall out because he's an insensitive brute.

GORGEOUS—As in the new boy in class with the blond hair, blue eyes perfect skin and broad shoulders. Perfect, in fact, if it weren't for the fact that he's only four foot nine. Mind you, if he wore high heels . . .

HEART—Which tends to be broken when you discover that the best looking guy in the disco happens to be attached to the sophisticated blonde who walks in as you're plucking up the courage to go and speak to him.

IRONING—What most guys can't, or won't do. You'd think most of them had *slept* in their clothes by their appearance. Scruffy, but lovable all the same!

JEALOUSY—The kind of envious green tinge that creeps across your face when you look at the blonde hanging on the arm of the George Michael lookalike you've had your eye on for weeks.

KISSING—Need we say more?

LOCK—A good solid one, preferably of padlock proportions, for the chastity belt that you slam your guy into while you're dragged off screaming on a family holiday to Southend.

MOTHERS—Cruel, heartless creatures who insist that you're in by ten o'clock on a Friday, even though everyone else will be out enjoying themselves until at least eleven.

TEDDY BEAR—For crying to when your guy finishes with you (See Elbow). Also for re-naming after whichever guy you fancy—so's you can cuddle up to him at nights!

UNDERSTANDING—What you'll need to account for all your boyfriend's faults. He may be clumsy, scruffy and invariably idiotic, but he's really special all the same.

VAIN—Another type of guy you'll want to miss out on. He'll be much too busy adjusting his hairstyle and smoothing back his eyebrows to pay any attention to you.

WHITE—The colour of your Knight in Shining Armour's charger. The one he'll sweep you off your feet onto. Also the one that will make you saddle-sore if you disappear too far into the distance with him!

XTRA' SPECIAL—Well, your boyfriend of course!

SMOOCHY—The kind of records that the DJ puts on towards the end of the disco. This signals the slow dances when the guy of your dreams will shuffle around with you in ever-decreasing circles, constantly stepping on your toes.

YES—What you'll say when the guy of your dreams ask you out to a candle-lit dinner for two. Sometimes followed by "... maybe", if he's talking about fish and chips underneath the lampost beside Joe's Takeaway.

ZZZZ—The sound you'll make during your beauty sleep that ensures all the guys'll be queuing up!

NABBED—Getting caught by your little sister, when you're kissing your guy goodnight. Made worse by the fact that she'll irritate you with little rhymes about it *all* week.

ORGANISED—What boys never seem to be. Watch him grin sheepishly when he admits he's forgotten his wallet at the cinema, or is late for the date because he was playing football with the lads and didn't have a watch with him .

POLITE—What you'll have to be to his parents when you meet them. Even though his father makes smutty jokes all the time you're there, and his mother makes not too subtle hints that no girl will ever be good enough for *her* boy!

QUESTION TIME—No, not the programme with Robin Day. It's what *your* parents will do to *him* when they meet him. As in, where is he taking you, and when will he bring you back? Tends to fluster most guys.

RAMBLE ON—The sort of thing that a guy will do when you're on your first date and he's walked you to your gate. He's trying to pluck up courage to ask for a goodnight kiss, so to stall for time he'll chatter incessantly about the most irrelevant subjects!

star daze!

Wonder why your guy acts the way he does? Check out his stars and all will be revealed!

GENERAL CHARACTER
— A boy born under Aries is a go-getter. He's not afraid to say what he thinks and do almost anything to get his own way. Be prepared for surprises when he's around. He's energetic and impulsive, often rushing into things without thinking! There's never a problem getting him out of his shell — he's never in it!

IN LOVE
— He hasn't the patience for a long cat-and-mouse game. He tends to grab what he wants, and that goes for girls, too! He's passionate and doesn't understand that sometimes a girl likes to be wooed. He likes to prove himself by taking girls out so if he fancies you, you'll soon know about it . . . he'll sweep you off your feet if you give him half a chance!

GENERAL CHARACTER
—Above all, a Taurus boy is reliable. He'll never let you down. If he said he'll be there at seven, he'll be there at seven. Always. Although Taureans are usually quite lovable and kind, watch out for his stubborn streak. If he thinks he's right, then nothing will change,

his mind. He's happiest with people and things he knows, which is why he can't bear to get rid of anything — especially his girl!

IN LOVE
— Taurus must be one of the most possessive signs of the Zodiac. He can fall very deeply in love, and he enjoys all the kissing and cuddling that goes with it. He's quite a cuddly character altogether! But just you try and even smile at another guy (even an old friend) and he'll go off in a huff. He wants you to belong to him alone.

GENERAL CHARACTER
— Geminis are great fun, the charmers of the Zodiac, but you can only trust them as far as you can throw them! The Gemini boy is chatty and witty, always the life and soul of the party, and manages to make the person he's talking to feel really special. He hates boredom and tends to switch friends and hobbies in a flash.

IN LOVE
— Gemini can be tricky to handle. Traditionally it's the sign of the two-timer. He doesn't mean to deceive you. When he says you're the only girl for him, he means it. It's just that he means it to whoever he's with at the time! He's like a little boy and you'll find it hard to stay angry with him for long — it's part of his appeal.

GENERAL CHARACTER
— The Cancer boy is one of the shyest. He's the ''boy-next-door'' type who's always there with a shoulder to cry on when you're feeling blue. He's loyal to his friends, but hates to show his feelings in public. Once you get a Cancer to come out of his shell you'll find out what good company he is and you'll have made the perfect friend!

IN LOVE
— Cancer is romantic. He'll never forget birthdays and anniversaries and he'll buy you presents galore. Being shy himself he'll try to protect you from the big bad world. He's tender and loving, but often goes head-first into romance. If you're the type who prefers a casual fling then he's not for you! He can be clinging and, 'cos he's sensitive, it's difficult to finish with him gently.

GENERAL CHARACTER
— Leos are born leaders, and love to feel important. A Leo boy will have a powerful personality — he'll want to lay down the law and have things his own way, and this can get on people's nerves sometimes! But he's generous

and warm-hearted enough to get away with it. He's full of good advice and ideas but leaves it to everyone else to get on with the details.

IN LOVE
— In love Leo expects to be adored. But if he fancies you you'll certainly not be left guessing! He can't take ''no'' for an answer and you probably won't want to refuse. He's the stuff that heroes are made of. He expects you to think only of him and he'll be just as true to you.

GENERAL CHARACTER
— The Virgo boy is usually quite clever. He's the bloke in your class who's always getting prizes without even trying! It's not that he's a swot, it's just that he loves finding out how things are

put together. Because he likes his mind to be tidy (so that the brain box works properly) he's also one of the smartest dressers around. He always keeps his cool.

IN LOVE — Like everything else about him his heart is ruled by his head. He doesn't fall often, and even when he does, he manages to keep it under control. He's old fashioned and might take you out loads of times before kissing you goodnight! Don't worry; he may be slow, but he's sure. And he likes to be sure — of you. But take care — he can be jealous and possessive, though he won't show it. This one's got hidden depths!

GENERAL CHARACTER — Like Gemini, Libra is the sign of charm. He's kind and easy-going, and likes a quiet life. If there's any trouble you can be sure he's the one trying to sort things out. He's too busy seeing everyone's point of view ever to take sides.

IN LOVE — Librans are really romantic. Your Libran boy will love cuddling up to you as you watch the sunset together. But he's not like Virgo, he'll be able to see your faults but they won't matter to him. It's you that's important. This doesn't mean he won't flirt sometimes. But he'll never two-time you — he's not that good a liar.

Continued over leaf. **79**

C·U·D·D·L·E-S·U·M
If you add it all up, the answer's love!

There are lots of different ways of finding out what people are *really* like — Astrology, Palmistry, handwriting, lumps, bumps, and so on! Well, forget them all — from now on, your number's up — or at least, *his* number is! Seems that *NUMBERS* can actually provide us with info about our attitudes to *LOVE*.

It might sound unlikely, but before you shrug it off as just another load of mumbo-jumbo, try this little experiment . . .

Relax and empty your mind . . . shouldn't be difficult should

it? Concentrate hard and pick any three numbers up to 9. For instance, suppose you decided upon 3, 4 and 7. Add these three numbers together and your total is 14. Now reduce this total to a single figure by adding the 1 to the 4, which gives you 5. The number you finish up with in this case, 5, is the key number of your secret love nature. Exciting isn't it? Of course, if the total of your original numbers is a single figure anyway — say, 1, 2 and 3 which equals 6 — then that's your key number.

Now read on . . .

Key No. 1

You're a born romantic . . . all hearts and flowers and fairy-tale music. And being a patient soul, you're prepared to wait some time for your knight on a white charger to gallop into your life and carry you off to his castle, although in your case it may be the boy down the road who sweeps you off your feet on to his rusty pushbike.

Sadly, life's not quite like it is in the story books, so you're likely to encounter quite a few disappointments where love's concerned. But at least you're sincere and once you meet this handsome hero of yours you'll probably live happily ever after (Sigh)!

Key No. 2

Love to you means security and — although you probably won't like to admit it — *money!* So hope your fella's got plenty of cash, 'cos you're not too keen on going dutch and you're not really into Women's Lib! In your book a guy must do the chasing — which is OK — but you might tend to miss out if you're too slow! While you're sitting looking pretty waiting for him to ask you out, more daring souls than you might jump the queue.

So live dangerously sometimes! Nothing ventured, nothing gained, we say!

Key No. 3

Your attitude to love is like your outlook on life — carefree and lighthearted. Heavy, intense relationships that tie you down make you feel uneasy. Live for today is your motto. But beware!

Although you attract the boys like bees round a honeypot, you're a bit of a flirt, so be careful you don't get stung. It may *seem* exciting to have boys fighting over you, but in reality it's no fun. Besides, it might be you that gets punched on the nose . . .

Key No. 4

You're loyal and faithful to the end, and it's quite possible you'll marry quite early in life, so start stocking your bottom drawer now! Your interests lie close to home where you feel secure. You can't bear to take risks, especially with money, so watch out you don't become a bit of a scrooge! And don't try telling your fella how to spend his cash! If he wants to buy a Cup Final ticket instead of a bunch of red roses for you — let him! Your turn will come!

Key No. 5

You demand a lot from love! But unlike some your wishes are at least realistic. It's just that there are rather a lot of them!

You crave excitement and enjoy travel. Because of this you are often attracted to boys from abroad, so you're a dead cert for that holiday romance. Everyone loves your lively personality and you'll never be short of admirers. But the guy you settle for in the long run will have to be a regular Superman . . . exciting and intelligent (and fairly rich if he's going to take you on all these exotic holidays!). Try getting a job as an air hostess. It's the best way to meet a millionaire.

Key No. 6

You're a motherly soul, and you like your fellas like your life — predictable! Nice, solid, down-to-earth, dependable-type guys are what you're looking for. Never one for rash impulsive actions, you hate being upset by changes of routine. But you're certainly faithful, and prepared to work hard at your relationships. Heaven help the boy who gives you the elbow, though — you find it very hard to forgive and forget, and once crossed, your anger knows no bounds!

Key No. 7

Come on, admit it, nobody's perfect and sometimes we just have to settle for second best! You expect too much from people, especially your guys! In fact, you're so fussy you're inclined to refuse every offer that comes your way, on the grounds that Mr Right might be waiting for you round the very next corner. But this cool image is guaranteed to put the boys off. And it's not really you, is it? Underneath you're not really sure that you can measure up to your own ideals, so this makes you pretty cagey about showing your true face to anyone! Just relax, everyone will respect the *real* you.

Key No. 8

Money . . . money . . . money! To you, the size of a guy's bank balance is more attractive than his face! But at least you know where you're going . . . and it's to the top!

Watch out though! All this longing for material wealth could get you into trouble. It can be tough, and lonely, at the top . . . just look at "Dallas" or "Dynasty". OK, they're rolling in it, but they're miserable! So, give the poor paper boy a chance — he's not exactly raking it in, but he does fancy you like mad.

Key No. 9

You're very forceful and dynamic, and not too keen to accept second best. After all, you're the sort of girl who can manage quite well on her own thanks! You're always on your soap box shouting your mouth off about something or other, so the quiet, shy type of boy would find you pretty frightening.

The boy for you would probably have to be completely deaf, or wear ear-muffs!

Continued from previous page.

Scorpio

GENERAL CHARACTER
—Scorpios are secretive and the Scorpio boy is best described as the strong, silent type. Scorpios try and hide their feelings but that doesn't stop others sensing their passionate nature. This telepathy also means that he seems to know what you're thinking before you've even thought it yourself!

IN LOVE — Scorpio isn't keen on Women's Lib. In love it's definitely he Tarzan — you Jane! If you're the type of girl who likes being dominated then this is the guy for you. He may seem secretive at first but this is just a cover for his sulky nature. If he feels there's any cause for jealousy watch out for the sting in his tail.

Sagittarius

GENERAL CHARACTER
— He's easy-going, playful, sweet-tempered and energetic. The ideal bloke! He loves to be on the go — shark-fighting, exploring, playing sport, mountain-climbing, anything which gives him space and freedom. His good nature means he usually gives people the benefit of the doubt.

IN LOVE — Sagittarius is a heartbreaker. It's not because he's a flirt but just that space and freedom are important to him. Romance ties him down and he's not ready for that. Some say he wants to have his cake and eat it! But if he's the guy for you let him have his freedom — he'll always come back!

Capricorn

GENERAL CHARACTER
— The most important thing to a Capricorn is his work. He has a serious nature and concentrates on things for hours on end. Lesser mortals tend to get bored with this behaviour so his friends tend

to be of a similar type. Whooping it up isn't for them! But even a serious Capricorn needs a change sometimes.

IN LOVE — He's slow to fall, but once he's fallen, that's it! It takes a lot to make him stray from the straight and narrow. He wants a steady relationship with a girl he can talk to. Of all the signs, Capricorn is one of the most faithful. You can depend on your Capricorn boy — if you can stay awake!

Aquarius

GENERAL CHARACTER
— This one is full of bright ideas — only half of which come to anything. He likes to get involved in causes such as CND, and he gives everything he's got to something he considers worthwhile. Ideas, places, people — everything attracts him. He'll never get caught in a rut!

IN LOVE — He believes in being faithful. But he seems a bit stand-offish and cool. The trouble is he's too busy saving the world to have any time left for you! Prepare yourself for an uphill struggle with this bloke or try and convince him you're a worthy cause.

Pisces

GENERAL CHARACTER
— He's dreamy and sensitive. His emotions are too near the surface. But if he gets angry quickly, he laughs just as easily. He hates suffering, especially animals being badly treated. The thought of a bullfight or a fox hunt can have him in agony. His sensitive nature means he is interested in the supernatural and may even have second sight!

IN LOVE — He's emotional and likely to be in love most of the time. He lives for the heartache of being in love. If there's no girl on the scene he'll pick one out and happily wallow in unrequited love, worshipping her from afar for months on end.

It's a WINNER!

ARE YOU A KNOCK-OUT WHEN IT COMES TO GETTING THE LAST WORD?

WHEN your boyfriend comes out with a really cutting comment, are you ready right away with a cool, snappy reply — or do you just start throwing things?

Y'know the situation. You and he are in the middle of a row that blew up over nothing at all. Suddenly, he turns round and yells, "I'm sick of the way you go on nagging! None of my mates have this problem!"

Instead of coming out with a snappy, put-down remark that'll bring him back to his normal, nice senses, you promptly burst into tears and rush out of the room saying you never want to see him again!

Familiar picture? We've all gone through it. It's only afterwards, when you're fuming into your box of tissues upstairs, that you think of cutting little come-backs.

Of course, trouble comes all the time — like when you've just bought what you consider to be *the* most amazing outfit, and he doesn't like it!

"You're not actually going to go out in that, are you?" he'll laugh sarcastically.

"No," you can smile sweetly. "I'm wearing it to sleep in. Goodnight!"

Getting the last word *always* makes you feel better. But finding the last word at the precise moment you *need* it isn't easy.

There's the sort of situation where he's with a crowd of his mates and is busily going on about how you can never make up your mind about anything.

"Oh yes, I can," you smile. "It's just that *my* mind isn't the same as your mind — it's better!"

Or if he suddenly wrinkles his nose and demands, "What's that nasty smell?" (when he knows perfectly well it's your new perfume because you've been telling him about it for twenty minutes!) — pause, sniff the air seriously, then murmur, "Your after-shave, I think!"

Other good interchanges include:

HIM: Now I feel a fool! (After he's been proved wrong about something.)

YOU: Yes, you look it!

HIM: You think more of your cat/dog/budgie/stereo than you do of me.

YOU: *It* thinks more than you do!

Y'see, it's all a matter of quick thinking! And there is one *other* situation where a handy quip at the right time can shut a whole *bunch* of fellas up!

That's when you suddenly discover you have to walk past about six of them, who all start shouting and whistling at you.

Muttering, "Drop dead!" under your breath will just make matters worse, because that's what they're *expecting* you to say. They're also expecting you to rush on blindly, blushing like mad, and with any luck (from their point of view!) tripping over your feet!

Instead, slow down. Walk calmly. Don't look at them. Once they're within earshot, fix the whistling ones with a pleasantly sarcastic smile and murmur, "How nice! Joining a choir?" — then walk on.

At least they'll go quiet for thirty seconds!

FEED
that body!

RAID THE KITCHEN

FOR THESE

BEAUTY TIPS!

Don't just sit there munching your way through the kitchen cupboard, bemoaning the fact that you're too broke to buy any cleanser or toner this month. Now's the time to discover the double life the food in your kitchen leads ... after all, it's not just for eating, you know! Food can be used in a number of ways to make you more beautiful. Read on for our top-to-toe hints!

RUN OUT OF SHAMPOO?

Beat two egg yolks into a cup of warm water, shampoo into your hair and leave for ten minutes. Rinse thoroughly afterwards.

If your hair is very greasy, try this one — beat four whole eggs in a cup. Apply to your hair, working in well with your fingers. Leave on your hair for at least 15 minutes and then rinse thoroughly. Make your final rinse one of cold water mixed with cider vinegar for a lasting shine!

NO CONDITIONER LEFT?

Beat two eggs in a cup and carefully add a tablespoon of olive oil, glycerine and cider vinegar. Apply this after you've shampooed your hair and leave on for at least 20 minutes. Then rinse with lots of water until hair is squeaky clean. This is a protein treatment and suits all types of hair.

If your hair is especially dry, or out of condition, try this one. Beat one egg, one tablespoon vinegar and two tablespoons of vegetable oil together. Work the mixture well into your scalp and hair, leaving it for at least 15 minutes. You'll have to shampoo afterwards, but it will give your hair a glossy shine!

HAIR LOOKING A BIT DULL?

Boil parsley in water for twenty minutes, strain off the parsley and use the water as your final rinse. If you have natural colours in your hair which only show up in sunlight, try simmering a handful of nettles and use the water as a final rinse. Not only will it bring out the colour of your hair, but it will add body, too!

FACE NEED A PICK UP?

Give yourself a face mask! You can use a variety of ingredients for this, and all should be left on for at least 20 minutes and then *thoroughly* rinsed off. Try crushed strawberries mixed with oatmeal or a mashed cucumber on its own. If your skin is oily, beat the white of an egg and add a drop or two of lemon juice. For dry skin, beat an egg yolk with a few drops of cider vinegar and a little vegetable oil.

RUN OUT OF TONER?

This is a bit more complicated, but it does work! Steep two cups of raspberries, one cup of rose petals and one teaspoon of honey in two pints of cider vinegar. Cover this mixture with a lid and leave for one month to work properly. When the time's up, carefully strain the liquid into a screwtop bottle and dilute with an equal part of distilled water. Store in the fridge to keep extra fresh and use with a cotton wool pad.

NO MOISTURISER?

You'll have to buy lanolin from a chemist, but all the other ingredients are simple enough. Melt one tablespoon of lanolin in a bowl over water. Then add one tablespoon of powdered oatmeal and, when the mixture is smooth, add half a cup of strawberry juice and beat until creamy. Sounds delicious, doesn't it?

If strawberries are too expensive, try this one. Heat half a cup of lanolin over water in a bowl and wait until it melts. Then add one cup of chopped lettuce and blend together. Remove from heat and lightly perfume with a few drops of rose oil. Strain before using or you'll get bits of lettuce everywhere!

CHAPPED HANDS?

Fill the sink with hot, soapy water and then smear your hands with olive or vegetable oil. Now plunge your hands in the water, working the oil in all the time. Pat hands gently dry with a soft towel afterwards.

NO CUTICLE REMOVER?

Mix together two tablespoons of pineapple juice, two egg yolks and half a teaspoon of cider vinegar. It will look awful, but soak your nails in it for at least half an hour. If you put this in the fridge it will last for a few more treatments — make sure you label it, though!

RUN OUT OF SUN TAN LOTION?

Peel a cucumber and wash it, straining the juice into a jar. Add half a teaspoon of glycerine and half a teaspoon of rose water to this and mix thoroughly. Store in the fridge and smear on liberally in the sun!

SUNBURNT?

Beat an egg white, 1 teaspoon of honey and half a teaspoon of witch hazel together until the mixture is smooth. Put in the fridge and use directly on bad sunburn.

LONELY

THIS

CHRISTMA

THE house felt empty, and so did I. There wasn't a Christmassy feeling, and yet everything was there, the same as last year. In the corner of the living-room the silver tree, dressed in tiny lights, glowed and twinkled. The ornaments I'd hung on the branches twirled in the draught from the open kitchen door, and silver angels' wings reflected the pink and pale blue and soft green of the lights.

"Isn't it lovely?" I'd asked John, this time last year.

"Fantastic!" He'd grinned. "But y'know you're talking to a Christmas freak. I'm like a kid over Christmas. I get so excited, just as if I was still five years old and waiting for a reply from the letter I sent up the chimney to Santa. I don't want to grow out of it!"

"Don't then! Be a kid for ever." I'd giggled, taking the hand he stretched out for me. "It's the reason I'm crazy about you!"

And I was, too. I was like a kid myself last Christmas. A small child amazed at the first snowflake. He was my first love. I'd never felt anything like the warm feeling that John gave me. Christmas had been the right time for us to meet. There was so much love and happiness and laughter in the air. It seemed right for us to join in.

We'd shared it excitedly, from our first meeting at the college Christmas fair, when I'd tried to sell him a bright red bobble hat I'd knitted, to the trek round the town with the carol singers when John held a lantern which kept going out, and I kept forgetting the words of the carols, because he was standing so dangerously close to me. Then there was the Christmas disco at college, when I'd blushingly asked if he'd like to go with me.

That's the night he kissed me, gently, lingeringly, under some stray mistletoe. That night. A year ago. The night he told me that he was just a big kid, who never wanted to grow up.

I loved that. I loved the craziness in him, the sudden stupid jokes and side-splitting laughter, the way he'd look at things with eyes wide in wonder as if he were seeing them for the very first time. He looked at me that way. He made me feel as special as his eyes told me I was, and he never stopped looking, and wondering and caring.

But, as I told my best friend, Chrissie, there was no pinning him down. Through the bright spring that his smile made brighter for me, and the long warm summer when we walked and talked and giggled in the sunlight, I was growing up fast. I was leaving college, my year's course was over. I was starting work, settling down.

"Good for you!" he told me. "Let me know when you're too settled down to love me!"

He wouldn't take anything seriously. He knew what I was driving at. I wanted some kind of promise. I wanted something to prove that our love would last for ever. I wanted to get engaged.

Chrissie was engaged. She'd got engaged in her last term at school. She and Don were saving up to get married when she was 18. She'd been my best friend right through school, and we'd kept in touch, even though our jobs were at different ends of the town.

Sometimes we'd go out in foursome, Chrissie and Do John and I. That's when t unfairness used to hit r hardest. It was obvious to r that John and I were easily much in love as those two we and perhaps more. We laugh more, talked more, enjoy each other's company so mu But he wouldn't prove he care

♥ ♥ ♥

"Well?" I finally asked hi at the beginning of this we as I dragged him towards display in the jewelle window.

"Very well, thank you." grinned. He had this infuriati habit of changing the subjec

"Aren't you going to ask what I want for Christmas? asked.

"No. I'm going to surpr you," he told me, smiling gentlest smile.

"Oh, John!" I sighed, annoy by the lurch of my heart. smile did things to me tha

couldn't control, and I didn't want to lose control, I had to tell him.

"I'd like an engagement ring," I said in a hard voice.

His smile faded, slowly. And then he squeezed my hand very tightly. Pulling me towards him, he looked down at me. It was the saddest look I'd ever seen in his eyes.

"Not *that* again, Marie," he whispered. "I've tried to explain. I'm not ready yet. I've got to finish my course at college, and then once I've found my feet . . . and anyway, I want to enjoy this . . ."

"What?" I snapped.

"This feeling I have with you. This easy feeling. It's a Christmassy feeling." He fumbled, trying to find the right words to tell me he cared.

I should have understood then. But I didn't. I couldn't. I broke free from his hand and the warmth of his smile. The look I gave him showed all the bitterness of my disappointment.

"OK, then, if that's what you want. I know what I want and I need someone who wants the same things I do. We're on different tracks," I told him.

I left him in the crowd of Christmas shoppers. I left him standing amongst the noise and laughter and the strains of Christmas music. I left him so that I could find someone to share a lifetime with.

There was already someone else. I'd met him at the firm's Christmas party.

He was tall and dark haired and smelt of after-shave. His name was Rick and he talked about football and his job. I was supposed to meet him again, and the rest of the crowd tonight at the café in town. He was what I wanted.

And yet . . . and yet I wondered whether he'd even realised that it was Christmas. He wasn't the kind of boy who'd notice angels' wings twirling in the draught on my silver Christ-

mas tree. He wasn't the kind of boy who'd look for mistletoe. He wouldn't romp in the snow like a six-year-old, trying to build a snowman before the snow melted. He'd grown up, he was past all that.

And suddenly, I didn't want that. In the emptiness of the house I buried my head in my hands and cried for the big kid who refused to grow up.

I remembered his eyes as they grew wide with wonder at silly things like Christmas trees. I wanted John. I wanted him, and all the happiness he'd given me. I wanted that much more than I wanted a shiny ring to show off to all my friends at Christmas.

"I thought you were going out tonight?" Mum said, coming in through the back door, stamping the slush from her boots. "Aren't you supposed to be meeting the crowd from work?"

"Well . . ." I sniffed, standing up, straightening out the

creases in the dress I'd bought to make me look grown-up, " . . . I thought I'd give it a miss. It wasn't anything special. I don't think they'll notice I'm not around . . ."

They wouldn't either. Rick wouldn't. He'd just talk to some other girl about football, and his job. He didn't think I was wonderful. I'd just thought I might be able to persuade him that I was, in time.

"So? What're you doing?" Mum asked, raising one eyebrow at me.

"I . . . I thought I might call round to see John . . ." I mumbled.

Mum smiled, a smile brighter than the lights on the Christmas tree, and hugged me, and let me cry on her.

"It's about time you came to your senses!" She laughed.

She'd always liked John. I'd always loved him. And I'd never stop loving him. It was an easy feeling we shared. A Christmassy feeling.

S. . . .

I loved the craziness in him, the stupid jokes and side-splitting laughter, the way he'd look at me. But sometimes love just isn't enough . . .

Continued from page 15

COVER-UP!
Very few of us have absolutely perfect skin. Even the models you see in magazines suffer from the odd spot and blemish — they just know how to disguise it better, that's all!

We've uncovered a few of those models' secrets especially for you . . .

Generally bad skin? Use a good foundation. Apply moisturiser first so that you have a smooth surface to work on, and then smooth on your foundation with a damp sponge. Choose a heavier type of foundation if your skin is especially bad, and remember to always finish off with a little translucent powder.

Broken or prominent veins? Try using Boots No. 7 Colour Corrective under your usual foundation. It will take away the redness — also helpful if you can't stop blushing!

Spots and blemishes? Buy a separate foundation or a concealer spot stick in a shade or two lighter than your usual colour. Use this on your blemishes or spots after moisturising and then smooth on your usual foundation. Make sure that you carefully blend in the two colours or it could look very obvious!

Greasy skin that shines? Choose a foundation especially made for oily skin, or one that is water-based as this will prevent a shine breaking through for ages. Powder your face thoroughly and remove any excess with a fat soft brush for a smooth finish.

Foundation too heavy? There are hundreds of foundations available, and they range from a light-as-air liquid to a heavy, thick solid pan stick type. If you're wary, why not use a tinted moisturiser? That's lighter, and has a dual purpose. You could always just use a spot concealer, of course, but remember to blend this in — and brush a little translucent powder over all your face for a more even look.

Buying a foundation is not difficult if you're prepared to spend a little time choosing it. Never judge a foundation's colour by the way it looks in the bottle or tube — ask for a tester and try a little on your face. After all, there's no point in testing it on your hand or wrist — it's your face you've got to match it up with!

FOR YOUR EYES ONLY!
Do you just brush on your eyeshadow any old way? Or do you know how to use it to make your eyes look bigger, less prominent, brighter? It can be done, you know — check out our eye-deas!

1) If your eyes are too small . . . Avoid outlining them with eyeliner or eye pencil becuse this just makes them look even smaller. You could use a pencil on the outer edge of your upper eyelids and smudge it with a cotton bud. Then apply a light eyeshadow on your eyelids, but use a darker shade towards the outer edges of the eye and up under the eyebrow. Finish off with a touch of white highlighter at the very outside edge of your darker eyeshadow.

2) Eyes too narrow? Don't use eyeshadow all over your eyelid, but leave space for a touch of highlighter in the centre of each lid. This makes any shape of eye look a little bigger so it's worth practising!

3) Eyes too close? If you have close-set eyes this tends to make them look smaller than they really are. To counteract this, use white highlighter all over your eyelids and up under your eyebrows. Be a bit heavier with the highlighter on the area of your eyelids nearest to your nose. Now brush on powder eyeshadow on the outer areas of your eyelids only and wing out the colour in an upwards direction. Remember to keep your eyebrows looking neat as this will make your eyes look bigger, too.

4) If your eyes are deep set . . . Instead of a dark eyeshadow, use a light one around your eye. Use ivory and white highlighter all over the eyelid again. Now add a little pale pink, but blend it in well. Add a touch of definite colour just under your eyebrows for effect, but don't ruin the look with excessive mascara. Never outline deep-set eyes with an eye pencil or eye liner — this only makes the problem worse.

5) Prominent eyelids? Apply a dark shade of eyeshadow on your eyelids, but a lighter colour under the browbone. Then blend in white highlighter on the very outside of your eye, under the eyebrow. A faint smudge of colour under the lower lashes helps, too!

6) If you want brighter-looking eyes...Use your usual eyeshadows, but lighten the area just under your eyebrows with an ivory-coloured highlighter. Also use this highlighter above your cheek bones and blusher — it will reflect the lighter colour above and make eyes look whiter and brighter!

UP LINES!

No matter how steady a hand you have, or what shape your lipstick, you won't get a professional-looking outline on your lips without a lip brush or pencil.

a) It may take a little longer the first couple of times, but you'll soon learn to pencil in, or draw in, your lipstick quickly. Use a lip pencil or a lip brush to carefully follow the natural outline of your lips — don't go right into the corner of your mouth, though. Then fill in the rest of your lip colour with a lip brush or with your lipstick alone.

b) If your mouth is too full, draw your line just within the natural outline, and this will make your lips took thinner. Another trick is to apply a darker lipstick in the centre section of your lips and a lighter shade on the outside.

c) If your lips are too thin you may feel that lipstick is a complete waste of time, but this is wrong. You can wear lipstick — and make your lips look fuller. Use a lip pencil to draw a line just outside your natural lip line and fill it in with a lipbrush and lipstick. Don't go too far outside your own lip line, though, or it won't look natural.

d) If your lips are uneven try a slightly lighter lipstick on the thin lip, and a darker one on the fuller lip.

PARTY TIME!

Our step-by-step guide to a completely new you!

1) Cleanse, tone and moisturise your face. Use soap and water if you prefer, but don't forget the moisturiser afterwards!

2) Wait a few minutes before dotting your foundation on both cheeks, your nose, chin and forehead. This gives your moisturiser time to sink in. Now use a damp sponge to smooth on your foundation, and be careful to blend it in under your jawline so that you don't have a harsh line where your foundation stops. If you have a spot or blemish use a spot concealer after the moisturiser and before the foundation.

3) Use a fat, soft powder brush to apply loose translucent powder all over your face. Then brush away the excess.

4) Now it's time to concentrate on your cheekbones. Brush your blusher on just above your cheekbones, and don't just apply it in rigid, straight strokes. Use the brush right up to your eyebrows to avoid harsh lines. Then lightly apply a shimmering highlight between your cheekbones and eyes, once again blending it in carefully.

5) Because this is a party face you can go wild with the eyes! Start with a light powdering of translucent powder all over the eyelid area. Then draw a line, either black or dark grey, with an eye pencil just under the lower lashes. Smudge this line with a cotton bud. Now use a pink eyeshadow on the area just under your eyebrows and bring it right down on to your lids. A smoky dark grey eyeshadow is next and it is applied on the outer area of the eyelid. Blend the pink and grey carefully where they meet. To make your eyes extra bright and interesting, apply a dot of white highlighter exactly in the centre of each eyelid.

6) Apply a thin coat of black mascara. Use an eyelash brush if there are any blobs, but otherwise leave to dry. Now apply a second coat, building up the lashes as you go.

7) Brush your eyebrows with an eyelash brush so that there is no powder trapped there. Smudge a little black eye pencil over them for extra emphasis.

8) Blot your lips with a tissue and dust a little powder over them. Now outline your lips with a lipbrush and then fill in the colour. Blot your lips with a tissue and apply again. Add a touch of clear gloss for effect.

Fifi, Robin, Melanie and Di . . . sound like the characters in a romantic novel, don't they? The only thing missing was the happy ending . . .

DOG DAYS

A SHORT STORY BY MARY HOOPER

ROBIN AYERS appeared out of his house when I was on my fourth — or it might have been fifth — trip down his road. I'd dicovered that the best thing about being a temporary dog owner was that it enabled you to walk wherever you wanted, whenever you wanted — and that included patrolling the street where the boy you'd fancied for three months lived.

He said hello to me and then his jaw dropped and he looked down at my side in amazement. "What's *that*?" he asked.

I was used to that sort of comment — I even had a set answer. "That's a dog," I said, slowly and clearly, and then I spelt it out: "D-o-g."

"I can see that! What sort of a dog, though?"

"A St Bernard," I said, cleverly falling into step beside Robin whilst making the move look completely natural.

"Wow! Yours?"

I shook my head. "No, I'm looking after it for my cousins — they've gone skiing."

He grinned. "I would have thought they could have done with a dog like that skiing. Aren't they the ones that come to sniff you out in the snow, with little barrels of brandy to revive you?"

I nodded and smiled, happy that I was the object of his attention, for once. Then my arm nearly got jerked out of its socket by the dog suddenly stopping by a lamp-post. I pretended to look elsewhere, praying that Robin wouldn't just walk on without me. After all, this was the first time I'd ever got him on his own — the first time we'd ever got into a proper one-to-one conversation.

"What's his name?" Robin asked — probably to cover up the embarrassed silence while we waited for the dog to finish whatever it was going to do.

"Well . . . er . . ." This was the even more embarrassing bit. "Fifi, actually."

"Fifi!" he exploded into laughter. Once he'd recovered sufficiently, he said again in a low, amazed sort of voice, "Fifi?"

"It's a girl," I said defensively. "You see, my aunt didn't want a St Bernard, he wanted a French poodle, and she said if she couldn't have a poodle, the dog would have to have a French poodle's name."

"Oh, yes?" he said, looking at me as if I'd cracked.

"We're not all mad," I said earnestly, and then we were off again.

"Heading for town?" Robin asked.

I nodded. A load of people at college had suggested we meet in the square every Monday of the holidays, just for something to do.

"I think the arrangement is a coffee, a

burger and then a walk," Robin went on. "What about Fifi, though?"

"Oh, she loves burgers," I said happily. So far, so good. We'd arrive at the square together, so we'd look like a real couple. After that, naturally, we'd sit together in the café, and later, even more naturally, he'd walk back with me. It was practically a date.

I'd just finished congratulating myself on the way this was turning out, when I noticed someone standing on the next corner looking at us coyly, head on one side.

"Come on, you two!" Melanie Hawkes cooed, and my heart sank. "Wasn't it eleven o'clock we were supposed to be meeting?"

She looked at Fifi and clasped her hands together. "What a simply *gorgeous* dog!" she cried. She took a few little running steps towards us. "Isn't he just adorable! What's your name, my petal?"

Fifi looked at her coldly. She can sense a rival a mile off.

"*Her* name's Fifi," I said firmly.

Melanie tittered smugly. "I don't believe it! What a scream! Oh, it's just too, too silly!"

She began to walk along with us — on Robin's side.

"It was quite a good idea to all meet, wasn't it?" she said, smiling at us both in a particularly sickly manner. "Mind you, I don't know how many will turn up. Maybe it'll just be you and Fifi and me and Robin!"

I glowered at her. The way she'd coupled the names hadn't been lost on me. "Kill!" I whispered to Fifi through clenched teeth, but she didn't seem to hear me and instead sauntered off to another lamp-post.

"Oh, how embarrassing!" Melanie cried. "I always think that dogs doing

things — you know! — in the street is *so* cringe-making. That's why I'd never have a dog." She looked at me self-righteously, willing me to go red, and I promptly did so. Fifi moved off again.

"Maybe we can all go across the common for our walk," Melanie said. "The weather forecast says sun — we could be lucky."

"Good idea," Robin said.

We reached the square. I was miserably aware of her chatting away to Robin as if she owned him — and saying cute things like she loved snow because making snowmen was such fun.

There were five people from college waiting in the square: two sisters, a large person in an even larger duffle coat who might have been a boy or a girl, and Nina and Malcolm, a couple who'd been going out together for ages.

Melanie saw her chance. "Let's go for a coffee now to warm us up!" she said, putting a hand on Robin's arm. Fifi growled.

We all walked across the square — Melanie in front with Robin and everyone else behind making a fuss of Fifi.

We'd just reached the café and I'd just decided that I'd make one last, desperate effort to push towards the front to make sure I got a seat next to Robin when Melanie turned and fixed me with a look of acute sympathy. I had an acute sensation, too . . . a deep desire to smash her teeth down her throat.

"I'm afraid you can't come in, Di!" she said with as much smarm as she could muster. "Positively no dogs, it says."

I looked at her bleakly, then pushed my way to the front and read it for myself.

"Oh," I said, and swallowed bravely. "Well, don't let me st . . ."

Before I'd even got the words out, Melanie was opening the door and ushering everyone in. "Coffees, everyone?" she cooed. "Maybe we'll see you later, Di. On the walk, perhaps?"

Fifi whined and I blinked rapidly, hoping I wouldn't cry in front of everyone. This was it, then — Melanie Hawkes had struck again, snatching Robin out of my arms at the final moment.

"Goodbye," I said in a small voice, and I went to walk away, but Fifi wouldn't budge.

"Hey, Melanie!" Robin said suddenly, halfway through the door. "Hold that coffee, will you? I think I'll go for a walk with Di."

I blinked some more — and through the window I saw Melanie's face as it changed from triumph to fury. "But . . . but . . ." she spluttered.

Robin let the door close behind them all, turned his collar up and looked towards the sky.

"I thought I'd come with you," he joked, "because if it's going to snow, I'd rather be with the mountain rescue dog."

"I see," I said solemnly.

"Come to that, I'd rather be with the mountain rescue dog's owner," he added, smiling.

I positively beamed back and we began to walk across the square towards the common. Our hands touched and linked and Fifi turned and seemed to look at us approvingly. I'd never seen an overweight St Bernard in the rôle of Cupid before, but even without a bow, arrow or cherubic face, I thought, she was managing rather well . . .

On The HAIRWAVES!

STEP-BY-STEP TO D.I.Y. HAIRSTYLING

DO you always come out of the hairdresser's feeling a little bit sad? Sad that your hair will never look as great as it does at that moment, 'cos you know your blowdrying technique is nowhere as good as your hairdresser's! It's especially hard if you've got a short, spiky style that *has* to sit right to look its best.

And it doesn't matter what styling gel or mousse you buy if you can't use it properly. Gels and mousses only work if they're given the chance, so we're here to show you exactly what to do to get the best from your hair.

We asked Ellen from Taylor Ferguson, and our model Phyllis, to show us a simple step-by-step guide to perfect styling.

1 Comb the hair into its style— using a wide-toothed comb so that the hair's not damaged in any way. Conditioner helps to reduce tangles, so remember to use it regularly.

2 Shake the mousse you're using very thoroughly. Then squeeze an application of mousse, about the size of a golf ball is a good guide, into the palm of your hand. Now apply it to your hair.

3 Comb the mousse, or gel, through your hair instead of just running your fingers across the top of your head. This helps the mousse to work more effectively.

4 Loosely dry the hair at this stage, either with a vent brush or your fingers. This is just to take away the excess moisture, so that you can style the hair properly.

5 Now start to shape the hair. A vent brush is a good brush for this styling because it has wide rows of bristles and allows lots of air through. Lift the hair as high as you can with each brush stroke. Keep the hairdryer moving over each section as you dry it, and don't let the dryer get too close or it could dry out and possibly burn your hair.

6 To give your hair extra lift, apply more mousse to almost dry hair. Dot the mousse where you'd like your hair to be spiky and work it down to the roots with your fingertips.

7 Now finish drying by using your fingers to give the hair a natural movement. Once again, lift the hair high as you can. If your hair is longer you could scrunch dry at this stage. All this means is using your fingers in a fist to 'scrunch' the hair together and styling your hair that way.

8 The finished result—and our model, Phyllis, is sure she'll be able to follow our step-by-step blowdrying guide at home herself!

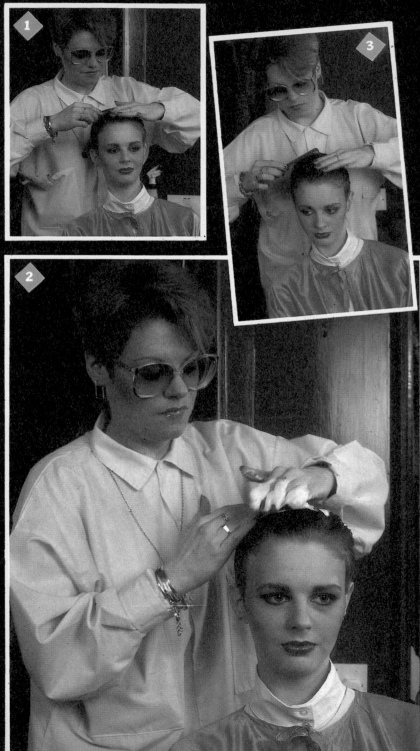

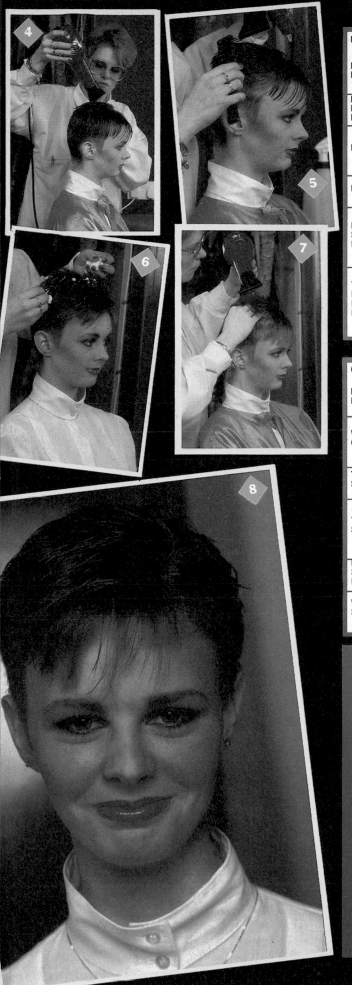

MOUSSES	Value for money	Holding power	Manageability	Pleasant fragrance	Comments
L'Oreal Freestyle Mousse	★★	★	★★	★★	One of the first mousses available. Not suitable for really spiky styles. A bit sticky.
Boots Country Born Styling Mousse	★★	★★	★★★	★★	Not too expensive. It needs hairspray for holding power.
L'Oreal Plix	★	★★★	★	★★	Very thick consistency. Available only from hairdressers. Hard to work in the hair and style, but does hold.
Insette Mousse	★★	★★★	★★	★★	2 kinds available — the extra hold is especially good for spiky styles.
Marks & Spencer's Hair Mousse	★★★	★★	★★	★★	Good value for money — and also available in 2 strengths. Try the stronger one if you want real holding power.
Taylor Ferguson's Hair Mousse — Extra Hold	★	★★★	★★★	★★	Available only from this hairdresser. Good styling hold — especially for spiky haircuts. Not at all sticky. 2 types — normal and extra hold.

GELS	Value for money	Holding power	Manageability	Pleasant fragrance	Comments
Boots Country Born Setting Gel	★★	★	★★	★★	A bit flaky. Needs hairspray to really hold hair in style.
Wella High Hair Gel	★	★★★	★★★	★★	Available from hairdressers only. Expensive. Really holds the hair in place. Doubles as a wet gel.
Tesco's Hair Setting Gel	★★	★	★★	★★	Only offers average holding power. Easy on your purse, though.
Tressemme´ 4 +4 Styling Glaze.	★	★★★★	★★★	★★★★	Available from hairdressers only. Very expensive. Good for very structured styles — can be diluted for ordinary hairdrying.
British Home Stores — Je Vive! Hair Gel	★★★★	★★★	★★★	★★★	Holds most styles. Definite value for money here!
Vidal Sassoon's Styling Gelle	★	★★	★★★	★★★	Good if you want a soft, bouncy style. Not firm enough for spikes, though.

It's not easy choosing hair products when there are so many on the market nowadays. And how do you decide between a mousse or gel in the first place?

Check our charts for a rough guide as to what each product is like; but don't forget that everyone's hair is different, and what suits someone else may not suit you. Your best bet is to try two or three different types to find the ideal mousse or gel for you.

Gel tends to be more economical, but some girls find mousse easier to use. Gel doesn't really work on long, straight hair, but you can use mousse to scrunch-dry it into shape. Short, spiky hairstyles can look good with mousse or gel. Try adding mousse to short dry hair to give a style a completely new look—it works just like wet gel! And remember to apply the gel or mousse as close to the roots as you can for the best effect. Mousse works especially well on hot hair, so try applying it right at the end of your hairstyling for extra effect.

Gels and mousses can actually do your hair a lot of good because they protect it from the damaging heat of a hairdryer, but try to give your hair a rest every now and then as they can also cause a flaky scalp.

It's not a good idea to use hairspray as a substitute for gel or mousse, though. It will hold your hair in place, but it will also cause breakage and damage if you continually blowdry over it. Don't overdo the backcombing, either—it will only leave your hair in very poor condition.

Oh, and one last word about gel . . . keep your eye on yours when your boy's around—more and more boys are using it now and you can't be too careful!

Hair and make-up by Ellen at Taylor Ferguson.

EAT *a treat!*

Spring a few surprises on your family this year —

here are four main dishes and four "puddings" — and

each makes up a seasonal meal you can put

together simply and sensationally!

autumn appetizers
PIZZA

winter warmers
(Ingredients for four throughout.)

CHILLI CON CARNE

30 ml/2 tablespoonfuls oil
1 large onion, chopped
2 garlic cloves, crushed
125 g/4 oz. bacon slices, chopped
½ kg/1 lb. minced beef
1 x 400 g/14 oz. can red kidney beans, drained
2 teaspoonfuls chilli powder
1 tin of tomatoes

Method:
Heat the oil in a saucepan. Add the onion, garlic and bacon and fry for 5 minutes. Add the beef and fry for a further 5 minutes or until it loses its pinkness. Stir in the remaining ingredients. Cover and simmer for 1 hour.

BLACKCURRANT FLUMMERY

1 packet lemon jelly
300 ml/10 fl. oz. boiling water
60 ml/4 tablespoonfuls blackcurrant syrup
150 ml/5 fl. oz. evaporated milk
150 ml/5 fl. oz. plain yoghurt
8 slices crystallised lemon

Method:
Dissolve the jelly in the water, stirring constantly. Put aside until it begins to set. Divide between two bowls. Beat the milk into one and the yoghurt into the other. Spoon a little of each mixture into four serving glasses and chill until set. Decorate with the lemon slices.

spring surprises

HAM AND PASTA SALAD

225 g/8 oz. macaroni
350 g/12 oz. cooked ham, chopped
225 g/8 oz. Bel Paese cheese, chopped
4 celery stalks, chopped
5 spring onions, chopped
15 ml/1 tablespoonful mustard
225 ml/8 fl. oz. mayonnaise
Salt and pepper
2 hard-boiled eggs, chopped
2 tomatoes, cut into wedges

Method:
Cook macaroni in boiling, salted water for about 8 to 10 minutes, or until soft. Drain, then cool. Put ham, cheese, celery and spring onions into a salad bowl. Stir in the macaroni. Stir the mustard into the mayonnaise and season to taste. Stir into the salad and toss well to coat. Garnish with the chopped eggs and tomato wedges.

MANDARIN DREAM

1 x 450 g/1 lb. can mandarin oranges, drained
50 g/2 oz. flaked almonds
225 ml/8 fl. oz. sour cream
30 ml/2 tablespoonfuls chopped crystallised ginger

Method:
Mix the oranges, almonds and sour cream together. Sprinkle over the crystallised ginger and chill for 15 minutes.

summer sensations

TUNA STUFFED TOMATOES

4 large, firm tomatoes, halved and de-seeded
2 hard-boiled eggs, finely chopped
1 x 200 g/7 oz. can tuna, drained and flaked
10 ml/2 teaspoonfuls capers
5 ml/1 teaspoonful chopped fresh parsley
45 ml/3 tablespoonfuls mayonnaise
Pepper
4 stuffed olives, halved

Method:
Turn the tomato shells upside down to drain. Meanwhile, put all the remaining ingredients, except the olives, in a small bowl and mix well. Pile the mixture into the tomato shells and garnish with the olives.

STRAWBERRY WHIP DRINK

½ kg/1 lb. strawberries
900 ml/1½ pints milk
225 g/8 oz. ice-cream
50 g/2 oz. sugar
2.5 ml/½ teaspoonful vanilla essence
Ice cubes
75 ml/3 fl. oz. double cream, whipped
4 whole strawberries to garnish

Method:
Rub strawberries through sieve into a bowl, beat in the milk, ice-cream, sugar and vanilla essence. Or alternatively, mix to a purée in a blender. Put some ice cubes into four tall glasses. Pour over the puréed mixture and top with a generous swirl of cream. Put a strawberry on the top of each glass.

250 g/8oz. Allinson's Wholewheat flour
1 teaspoonful baking powder
1 egg
½ teaspoonful salt
45 g/1½ oz. margarine
¼ pint milk
PLUS
1 teaspoonful olive oil
2 tablespoonfuls tomato purée
1 teaspoonful mixed herbs
50 g/2 oz. salami — sliced
100 g/4 oz. mozzarella cheese — cubed or grated
25 g/1 oz. red or green pepper — sliced
Black and green olives
Anchovies
Capers

Method:
Sift dry dough ingredients into a bowl and rub in fat to fine breadcrumbs consistency. Mix to a soft dough with lightly-beaten egg and milk and knead lightly until smooth. Turn dough on to a floured board and roll out to ½-¾ of an inch thick. Place on a greased pizza pan or baking sheet. Brush over with olive oil, spread with tomato purée, sprinkle over half the mixed herbs. Arrange salami, olives, anchovies, peppers and capers, sprinkle with remaining herbs. Finish with cheese. Cover loosely with polythene and leave in a warm place for 15 minutes. Bake at 425 deg. F., 220 deg. C., Gas Mark 7, for approximately 20 minutes.

CARAMEL BANANAS

50 g/2 oz. butter
150 g/5 oz. brown sugar
4 large bananas, sliced
50 ml/2 fl. oz. single cream
600 ml/1 pint vanilla ice-cream

Method:
Melt the butter in a frying pan. Add the sugar and stir until it has dissolved. Stir in the banana slices so that they are thoroughly coated. Cook for 5 minutes or until the bananas are tender. Stir in the cream. Divide the ice-cream between four glasses and spoon over the banana mixture.

Over and Out!

You've found out that your boyfriend has been seeing someone behind your back. Either that or he ignores you, or doesn't phone you for hours on end, or . . .

Well, whatever it is, it's time to ditch him. And if he's been rotten to you, then retaliate in kind . . . !

HOW TO BREAK THE NEWS

Say it with flowers: By far one of the most touching ways to tell him it's time you should part company. A wreath would be quite suitable, either that or a triffid. He'll probably get the idea.

Say it with a phone call: Or "just call to say you hate him." It's the subtle way to tell him that he's not for YOOO-HOOOO! The good thing about a phone call is that you don't actually see him. That means your resolve — and heart won't melt when you see the look in the deep brown eyes . . . !

Say it in a letter: The opposite of a love letter — a hate letter. Well, possibly a deep dislike letter.

However you define it, there's only one way of writing it . . . badly! The content's unimportant, what matters is the presentation. Use that old, leaky felt-tip pen, the one that's the disgusting colour of green. Be sure to spell and punctuate badly and carefully smudge dirty fingerprints all over it.

The finishing touch to any effective "Dear John . . ." letter is the lingering fragrance. Instead of delicate scent, try "Eau de Disinfectant." And a faint, soapy smell will tell him that he hasn't cleaned his act up.

Say it publicly: And make it very public by putting an advert in the local paper. Beside all the notices saying:

"Sweetie-Pie, Love you madly. Squirrel Nutkin xx."
You can have,
"Rat-face, Think you stink. You know who!"

Say it sky-wise: Emblazon it across the cloudless blue by hiring an airliner from British Airways. The jet trail can spell out your malicious message. After all, it's the better way to un-tie.

IMPORTANT government health WARNING: Taking some of this advice could SERIOUSLY DAMAGE YOUR GOOD REPUTATION!

DROPPING SUBTLE HINTS

Spend all night chatting to the local hunk at the disco and when your guy comes wandering over, assure him that you and the hunk are just good friends, "Aren't we, Butch?"

Get your mate to answer the phone when he calls and say, "Oh, you must be Carlos, she hasn't stopped talking about you since you spent that fortnight together in Benidorm . . . I see, you're not Carlos!"

Tell him you're taking up knife throwing and would he mind helping you with your practice? If he'd just put this apple on his head . . .

Go overboard on the current craze for wearing men's clothes and start using men's after-shave. Just splash it all ovah.

Insist on taking your gran/little bruv/pet gorilla with you on every date.

Tell him to get lost.

Every time he tries to hold your hand or give you a peck on the cheek, slap him across the face and say as sweetly as possible: "I'm not that kind of girl."

Tell him that your family is off to Australia and although you won't actually be going for ten years or so, you thought you'd better split up now just so you can both get used to it.

As he puts his arm around your shoulder, snuggle into him and say: "Oh, David." This will work only if his name isn't David.

Get your mum to answer the phone: "If that's Frank she's washing her hair, if it's Stuart she's round at her mate's, if it's Mike she'd like you to pick her up in half an hour."

Scare him off by hinting at a serious relationship. This is guaranteed to drive off even the most persistent guy. Suggest that he comes along to your family's annual gathering, 'cos if he doesn't, he'll never be accepted as one of the family. Either that or sit beside him looking dreamily into Pronuptia catalogues and ask him to work out how long it would take to save up for a wedding dress if you pooled your pocket money.

Tell him that you have a terrible disease that is very contagious and may well be fatal (neglect to mention that it may take 70 years for the virus to take effect).

PYJAMAS

The trendiest parties in town are the pyjama ones, so grab your dad's old ones or rush out and buy your own.

Pyjamas by British Home Stores.

'ELLO 'ELLO 'ELLO

Don't let the party noise get out of hand, 'cos if a neighbour complains, the police are bound to pay you a visit.

If you don't turn it down after they've warned you, then you or your parents can be arrested for breach of the peace!